A NEW THEORY OF BEAUTY

Guy Sircello

A New Theory of Beauty

*Princeton
University
Press*

Copyright © 1975 by Princeton University Press
Published by Princeton University Press, Princeton and London
All Rights Reserved

Library of Congress Cataloging in Publication Data will
be found on the last printed page of this book

Publication of this book has been aided by
the Andrew W. Mellon Foundation

This book has been composed in Monotype Garamond

Printed in the United States of America
by Princeton University Press, Princeton, New Jersey

TABLE OF CONTENTS

v

TABLE OF CONTENTS

ACKNOWLEDGMENTS

I am grateful for the help and support given to me while I was writing this book by my colleagues in the Philosophy Department at the University of California, Irvine: Jill Buroker, Richard Holzman, Karel Lambert, A. I. Melden, Nelson Pike, Gerasimos Santas, David Smith, William Ulrich, and Peter Woodruff. My thanks go also to those many students of mine who always insisted that the nature of beauty is an important philosophical topic. I was finally convinced.

A NEW THEORY OF BEAUTY

1. *Beauty and the Twentieth Century*

Beauty is all around us in things both natural and artificial. All sorts of human beings in all varieties of cultures enjoy beauty. But despite the efforts of thousands of years the idea of beauty has not yet been understood. These are good enough reasons for thinking about beauty again.

Twentieth-century Western civilization is paradoxical because although it has produced beauties in abundance, it has not paid serious attention to understanding beauty. Many of its artists either ignore beauty or spurn it. Although they have not been able to stamp it out, they have often succeeded—albeit not so often as legend pretends—in making beauty artistically beside the point. Intellectuals and academics, who might have been expected, because of tradition, to take the idea of beauty seriously, have usually been overimpressed by contemporary artistic programmes and have decided that beauty is culturally irrelevant, that "nobody" talks about it anymore. This despite the fact that the characteristic artifacts of our time—like the airplane and the freeway interchange—are among the most beautiful the world has ever known; that a characteristic religion-surrogate of our time—spectator sport—idolizes beautiful bodies in beautiful motion; and that almost anybody on the street is willing to talk about these beauties. Yet even ordinary, nonintellectual, and semi-educated people have assumed, against the testimony of their own experience, that beauty is only "subjective" and therefore cannot be meaningfully discussed. In this they have been supported by important philosophers, artists, and critics who have—groundlessly—come to the same opinion.

These various rejections of beauty are symptomatic of what is admitted on all sides to be this century's great problem of morale. This malaise goes by various names; "alienation" is currently its most chic name. It is, most generally described, the feeling of being a stranger, of not being at home, in one's world. No doubt there are deep cultural causes of this feeling. But when we scorn beauty, or ignore it, or think we have lost it inside our heads, we have scorned, ignored, or apparently lost the best and most delightful part of our world. No wonder we feel alien in such circumstances.

Yet however people *feel*, the *fact* remains that we are not strangers in the world, not even in the world of twentieth-century civilization. A true theory of beauty will show this, for beauty is a part of the world, and human beings, enjoying beauty, fit the world as a hand fits a glove.

I merely assert the above propositions. I have no arguments for them even though I think they are true. The rest of this essay, however, contains extended arguments, both for a theory of what beauty is and for a theory explaining why we enjoy it. I believe the arguments are good and the theories new; and I hope, in addition, that someone might even see the relevance of them to my introductory remarks.

2. *Skepticism with Regard to Beauty*

Kant started it all by declaring that the judgment of beauty is not determined by concepts.[1] He meant that no criteria of beauty can be given in terms of features of the objects to which "beautiful" is applicable; and he thus opened the gates of sub-

[1] I pick on Kant only because his particular views have been so influential. But, as Jerome Stolnitz has shown in an interesting article, " 'Beauty': Some Stages in the History of an Idea," *Journal of the History of Ideas*, XXII (1961), subjectivism with respect to beauty had become a widely shared opinion among philosophers by the end of the eighteenth century.

jectivism. This form of skepticism with regard to beauty has dominated most of the up-to-date thought of the last two centuries. At a certain level of superficiality, the skepticism is reasonable. First, it's easy to see that no one has yet offered a clear enough or a comprehensive enough theory of beauty. Second, the task of finding a criterion of beauty seems, *prima facie*, beyond human powers. For just consider the range of objects to which beauty can be attributed: people, rocks, snakes, daisies, horses, trees, mountains, rivers, paintings, symphonies, buildings, spoons, books, chairs, hats. Confronted with this array, even the most intrepid theorist is likely to despair of uncovering features that all beautiful objects share and that constitute necessary and sufficient conditions for the correct attribution of beauty.

No one in his right mind, of course, would agree that, in general, if a job *seems* overwhelming and has never been done, there is compelling reason to conclude that it is impossible to do. Usually what is needed in such circumstances, we recognize, is more ingenuity and more will. We do not recognize this, anymore, about the quest for a criterion of beauty, because our will has been sapped. We hear from one side that the very search for necessary and sufficient conditions is perverse ("wrongheaded"); from another that it is reckless and irresponsible because it will take the mystery and splendor out of our experience of the beautiful; from another that in making such a search we lose integrity because we are merely aping "science"; and from another that in trying to put soft, aesthetic notions on the same footing as hard, scientific concepts we are being presumptuous. In the face of such tactics of intimidation, most persons who think about beauty at all nowadays are, I suspect, *glad* to believe that it is not determined by concepts. In our time, skepticism with regard to beauty is not the comfortless but brave conclusion of the man of reason, true to himself to the end. It is, rather, a welcome refuge for the beleaguered and fearful humanist who wants, above all, to be liked.

3. *Beautiful "Objects"*

The best way to refute skepticism is simply to provide a clear, comprehensive, and true theory that gives the criterion of beauty in things. The way to do that, however, is not to search for features common to all beautiful objects, for a moment's reflection will show that if we restrict our attention only to beautiful objects, we shall miss much of the world's beauty. Mountains, rivers, and symphonies may, in an attenuated sense, be called objects. But the starry night, the ridgeline of the Santa Ana Mountains against the morning sky, the way the Philadelphia Orchestra plays Strauss, the color of California hills in spring, a well-executed *arabesque penchée*, and the late afternoon sunlight reflecting off the waves are by no means objects. Of course, we *need* not construe "object" so pedantically. We could mean by "object" in these contexts merely anything denoted by the subject of a sentence in which "beautiful" is a predicate adjective. Let us, accordingly, enlarge the class of things we take to be objects. We will henceforth refer to members of this larger class as *"objects"*—with the scare quotes a part of the referring term. The class of beautiful "objects," then, includes much more than the class of beautiful objects.

With "object" so defined, however, skepticism looms even larger. The springtime hills are beautiful; their color is beautiful. Helen's skin is beautiful; the clearness of her skin is beautiful. But what do the hills and their color, or Helen's skin and its

6

clarity, have in common that makes them both beautiful? Indeed, what *could* a hill and a color (of anything), or skin and clearness (of anything), have in common? Not only do these things and their properties have nothing in common, but it looks as if such categorially different "objects" could not possibly have anything in common that would ground their beauty.

If, then, we ask what is common to all beautiful "objects," we seem driven to a hard skepticism. But must we, should we, ask precisely *that* question? We ask what Helen's clear skin and the green hills of spring have in common to make them beautiful. The question might have no answer, but at least the motive for asking it is reasonable: there is beauty in one thing here and beauty in a different and unrelated thing there, and we wonder how that can be. With the hills and their color, however, the problem is not that there is beauty in one thing here and also in an unrelated thing there and hence a total of two beauties that need to be accounted for. The beauty of the hills in spring could easily be *nothing but* the beauty of their color. Likewise, the beauty of Helen's skin could easily be *nothing but* the beauty of its clearness. There are not necessarily two beauties (that is, two instances of beauty) in each of these cases, but very possibly only one. So our inability to find anything in common between the things and their properties need not lead to skepticism—or at least lead to it any more convincingly than our inability to find anything in common between hills and skins.

4. *"Beautiful Properties"*

If in seeking a viable theory of beauty we cannot simply ask what features all beautiful objects share, on pain of missing some beauty, and we cannot ask what features all beautiful "objects" share, on pain of asking an unanswerable question, what questions *can* we ask in order to uncover the necessary and sufficient conditions of the beauty of things? I will come to an answer to this question indirectly by following a line introduced in the preceding section.

Under what conditions could we say that the beauty of the hills is nothing but their beautiful color and the beauty of Helen's skin is nothing but its beautiful clearness? We could say so, first, if we knew that *what is beautiful about* the hills is their color or (what I will take to mean the same thing) if we knew that they are beautiful *with respect to* their color. Similarly, we could say that the beauty of Helen's skin is just its beautiful clearness if we knew that *what is beautiful about* her skin is its clearness, that her skin is beautiful *with respect to* its clearness. But of course we can't say that the beauty of the hills is *nothing but* the beauty of their springtime green or that the beauty of Helen's skin is *nothing but* the beauty of its clearness, unless the hills are beautiful with respect to *nothing but* their green color or unless Helen's skin is beautiful with respect to *nothing but* its clearness. And if the hills are beautiful with respect to their green color *and* with respect to their soft look ("soft-lookingness"), and only these, then the beauty of the hills is nothing but the beauty of their green color and their soft look. In general, the beauty of an "object" X would seem to be nothing but the beauty of all its properties that are beautiful, or the beautiful properties of all those "objects," if any, with respect to which X is beautiful, or both.[2]

[2] This general statement, of course, can hold only for beautiful "objects" that are in fact beautiful with respect to properties. At this point in the discussion, it is certainly an open question whether all beautiful "objects" are beautiful in such a respect.

The point I am making about "beautiful" applies, analogously, to less controversial predicates. Take "red," for example. Suppose that we wanted a theory of redness and were faced with the following facts: the ball is red; the ball's surface is red; the color of the ball's surface is red. It is transparent in this situation that our theory need not account for three instances of red; the redness of the ball just *is* the redness of its surface, and the redness of its surface just *is* the redness of the color of the surface. So if our theory comprehended the color of the ball's surface, it would at once comprehend the redness of the ball and of its surface.

But, you ask, couldn't Helen's skin or the hills of home have beauty independent of the beauties of *any* of their respective properties? If so, it would also be possible for them to possess *no* beautiful properties and yet be beautiful. We would ask "What is there about the hills that is beautiful? With respect to what are they beautiful?" And a legitimate answer would be: "There is nothing about the hills that is beautiful; there is nothing with respect to which they are beautiful. They are, nevertheless, beautiful." I want to claim on the contrary that, at least for "objects" that are not themselves properties, such an answer is never warranted. That is, I am claiming that at least all beautiful "objects" that are not properties are beautiful with respect to some other beautiful "objects." I cannot, however, think of any convincing deductive argument that yields such a conclusion. My reasons for believing the claim are these: (1) For a great many beautiful "objects" we can indeed say what is beautiful about them by mentioning one or more of their beautiful parts, elements, or properties. Therefore, (2) it is not generally true that "beautiful" applies to all "objects" *in no respects*. Furthermore, (3) even of those beautiful "objects" about which we cannot specify the respect(s) in which they are beautiful, it is never impertinent to pose the questions "What about them is beautiful? In what respect(s) are they beautiful?" And this fact implies (4) that there might well be an answer to the questions, even if it does not *guarantee* that there is an answer.

The above considerations are enough for me. Yet I can sympathize with the temptation to deny the conclusion I draw from them. Driving to work this morning I caught sight of a gorgeous and unusual scene in which the nearby mountains were beleaguered by a storm, while the area around me was bright and the sky forming the "backdrop" for the mountain storm was radiantly clear. I did not know then, and do not know now, what about the scene was so beautiful. Then again, every morning I glimpse a view of the Irvine Campus, of the Engineering Building rising above Campus Park, that does not fail to strike me as beautiful when it is foggy. Still, I do not yet know what there is about that view that is so beautiful.

Experiences like these are not uncommon. They do not, however, show that there are beautiful "objects" that are beautiful in no respect, that have nothing beautiful about them. After all, I can go on asking myself what is beautiful *about* these mysteriously beautiful "objects." Why? One answer is that I am compulsively analytical and go on asking questions that would not bother most people. But that does not make my question absurd, as if I were asking for what does not exist for what could not be. In times past I have pressed the question until I got answers that were just right, were convincing. One day I glanced straight up the trunk of a eucalypt in my front yard and was struck by a beauty I could not fathom. I finally saw that from my angle the branches growing out from the trunk made a radial pattern that gave a beautiful "bursting" or "explosive" look to the tree that I had never noticed before.

Experiences like this constitute, of course, merely *empirical* evidence that if I keep wondering long enough about where the beauty of an "object" resides, I shall discover where. But, for better or worse, that's the best kind of evidence we have.

5. *The Job of a Theory of Beauty*

Now we can suggest a way of answering the question posed at the beginning of the last section. If certain "objects" are beautiful only with respect to certain other beautiful "objects," a maximally comprehensive theory of beauty need not concern itself with the former "objects." Furthermore, if the whole class of beautiful "objects" were divisible, without remainder, into a class of beautiful "objects" that are beautiful with respect to other "objects" and a class of "objects" with respect to which ultimately all the "objects" of the first class are beautiful, then a maximally comprehensive theory of beauty need be a theory solely of the beauty of the latter class of "objects." And if, finally, we could specify in a general way the class of such "objects," we would thereby simplify and clarify the job of constructing a comprehensive theory of beauty.

Note that the class of beautiful "objects" contains, on the one hand, objects in the most restricted and unproblematic sense of the term—e.g., stones and boxes—and, on the other, properties like *greenness, clarity, explosive-lookingness* (or, in English, *explosive look*). There are many other "objects," like clouds, persons, patterns, views, ways of performing, that may be more like the objects or more like the properties but are not indisputably like the one or the other. Now it appears to be quite universally true that if, of any beautiful "object" X, *which is not clearly a property*, we ask "With respect to what is X beau-

11

tiful?'' or ''What about X is beautiful?'' then either (1) we can answer the question by naming one or more beautiful properties or (2) we can apply the question again to what we put forward as an answer. Furthermore, we can continue applying the question until the answer is given by naming a beautiful property (or properties). Thus what is beautiful about the hills, say, is their greenness and their soft look. What is beautiful about Helen is, say, only her skin, and what is beautiful about her skin, say, is only its clearness. What is beautiful about my eucalypt, say, is only the radial pattern I see when I look up its trunk. And what is beautiful about that pattern, say, is only its ''explosive'' look. We have here, then, many diverse beautiful ''objects'': the hills, their greenness, their soft look, Helen, her skin, its clearness, my tree, its pattern, the pattern's ''explosive'' look. But it would appear that a comprehensive theory of beauty could do its job perfectly well if it could account only for the beauty of the hills' greenness and their soft look, the clearness of Helen's skin, and the eucalypt's ''explosive'' look. It seems, thus, that beautiful ''objects'' can be ordered in such a way—namely, by asking a certain question about all nonproperties—that beautiful properties acquire a privileged status in any theory of beauty.[3]

What we need at this point is a sufficiently precise determination of what counts as a property. The best tactic for now is simply to say that a property is whatever is signifiable by any adjectival word or phrase that can complete a sentence of the form X *is* _____. This stipulation lets into the range of properties more than we need or want, but it excludes much of the

[3] I admit to having no *argument* for this absolutely crucial step. I rest the claim on an ''inspection'' of the field of beautiful ''objects'' and on my own failure to find counterexamples to the proposition.

class of beautiful "objects." In any case, the class of properties we are interested in is further delimited by the requirement that they be *beautiful* properties. Thus, although "tiny," "late," "high," "pessimistic," and "dirty" all signify[4] properties, they are not, so far as I can see, properties that form part of the subject matter of a theory of beauty. This determination of "property" is more restrictive than most. For in sentences of the form *X is* ____ that are completed by adverbial phrases, such phrases do not signify properties. Hence *being over the hill, being next to Guatemala, being farthest from Mars* do not, for our purposes, count as properties. Nor do *being ripened, being wrought, being enhanced* count as properties, since they are signified by the past participles of verbs, not by adjectives, in sentences of the form *X is* ____. Likewise *leaping, gamboling in the meadow, radiating joy* do not count as properties because they are signified by the present participles of verbs in sentences of the form *X is* ____, thereby transforming the "is" from a copula into an auxiliary verb of the continuous present tense. This restricted notion of property may seem arbitrary, but reflection will prove that at least no beautiful properties are thereby excluded.

The phrase "beautiful properties" may bother some readers. Remember that the way we came to our present position was by first noticing that "beautiful" does apply to some properties—for example, a greenness and a clearness that make their objects beautiful. Now, of course, we have generalized the point. It may be that not *every* property brought to light by the question-asking procedure described above can, in some context or other, be said to be beautiful. But certainly most of

---

[4] "Signify," by the way, does not mean "name"; "dirty" *signifies* the property that "dirtiness" *names*.

them can; think of the beautiful trustfulness of her eyes, the beautiful mystery (mysteriousness) of the blue velvet she was wearing, the beautiful solid look ("solid-lookingness") of the bull against the sky, the beautiful stillness of *La Grande Jatte*. We need not insist on the general point, however. It is enough simply to say that a comprehensive theory of beauty need give an account only of those properties, whether in any context properly *called* "beautiful" or not, that can constitute what is beautiful about some beautiful "objects." When I say "beautiful properties," I shall mean such properties.

A much more fundamental point about the term "beautiful property" must be raised now. The term itself suggests that a beautiful property is to be considered beautiful "in general," that is, in any possible instance of it. Notice, however, that whenever we call a property "beautiful," we always apply the term to the property *as it is instantiated in a specified "object."* It is not greenness in general that is beautiful when the hills are beautiful. It is not clearness in general that is beautiful when Helen's skin is beautiful. It is not even clearness-of-skin in general that is said to be beautiful. It is the greenness *of those particular hills*, the clearness *of Helen's skin*, that is beautiful. And thus we say that there is *a* beautiful greenness in those hills and *a* beautiful clearness to Helen's skin. Therefore, calling greenness a beautiful property means only that it is *possible*[5] for it to be beautiful in some of its instantiations, not that it *is* beautiful in all of its instantiations.[6]

---

[5] Only possible, not actually the case. For if tomorrow all the "objects" beautiful with respect to their greenness were annihilated, greenness would still be a beautiful property.

[6] It could happen that at any given time all "objects" possessing a property might be beautiful with respect to that property. But it could not happen that every possible instance of a property might be beautiful with respect to it. Why this is so will become clear later.

14

Now since a comprehensive theory of beauty needs to account only for beauty of properties, it requires no more than finding what is common to all beautiful properties in virtue of which they are beautiful. Such an identification can proceed in several ways. We could, but need not, identify the *class* of beautiful properties in terms, naturally, other than their being beautiful. But even if we did, our job would not be done, for we would still have to distinguish the instantiations that make the properties beautiful in certain cases from those that do not. Now we could do so, of course, by identifying a class of "objects" that, possessing the properties, make those properties actually, and not only possibly, beautiful. Clearly, however, if this is what the theory required, there would be no advantage whatsoever to having reduced beauty of "objects" to beauty of properties; we would have come full circle to be faced with the original task of finding the common ingredient in all beautiful "objects."

Another apparently possible tack would be to identify a distinct *way of being instantiated*, so that a (possibly) beautiful property would be actually such when it is instantiated in that way rather than some other way. Unfortunately, this suggestion makes no sense to me. An "object" either instantiates a property or does not; the relationship of instantiation seems to be so absolutely simple and immediate that there could be no "room," as it were, for "styles" of instantiation.

There is only one way remaining—as far as I can see—for a theory to grab hold of properties-as-they-are-instantiated and distinguish the beautiful ones from the non-beautiful ones. That way is to distinguish, for all *F*, *a way of being F* in virtue of which, for all *X*, *X* is beautifully *F*, from other ways of being *F*. This is, in other words, what a successful theory of beauty *must* do. What a successful theory of beauty *might* also do—and what might thereby also make its necessary task easier —is to determine the domain of *F* to be a certain subset of the set of all properties as defined earlier.

All that a perfectly comprehensive theory of beauty need do, therefore, is to determine what, for all *X* and all *F* such that *X* is beautiful with respect to *F*-ness and such that *F*-ness is beautiful as instantiated in *X*, makes *X* *beautifully F*. In a way, that is an astounding conclusion, for we have always known that if *X* is *beautiful* with respect to *F*, then *X* is *beautifully F*, and vice versa. But we have never paid any attention to this adjective-adverb interchangeability. We have taken the adjectival form *beautiful* to be irreducible, treating it like any other adjective (even though very few other adjectives admit the same kind of adverbial transformation), and have assumed beauty to be a property of things, like yellowness or rectangularity.[7] And it was, of course, by following where that assumption led that I came finally to see that we might understand all the beauty there is by not considering beauty a property at all but a way "objects" have of being *F*, for all *F* (whatever the domain of *F* may turn out to be). I have been able to conclude, in other words, that the adverbial form *beautifully* (as it applies to adjectives) is the basic linguistic form for the subject matter of a general theory of beauty. Note, however, that this conclusion still does not leave us with any guarantee that a comprehensive and true theory of beauty is possible. All that I have accomplished so far is to specify—in a way I think has never been done before—what the job of such a theory is.

---

[7] Even philosophers like Plato and Plotinus, who are finally led to believe that the nominal form *beauty* is basic, and hence that beauty is essentially a substance and only accidentally a property, were led to this view by taking the adjectival form *beautiful* as, in some sense, an unquestionable given.

For all we know at this point, there is no way of being F that is a necessary and sufficient condition of any "object" beautiful with respect to F being *beautifully F*.

Another caveat should be entered here. Although a comprehensive theory of beauty can be given by a comprehensive theory of beautiful properties, it still might be necessary, in order to provide the latter, to reduce in turn the beauty of properties to the beauty of a special kind of property. In fact, it will be necessary to make such a reduction. Keep this in mind throughout the discussion of beauty of color. For there I shall be talking about properties-as-instantiated-in-a-specified- "object" that are themselves beautiful with respect to some further property or properties. Also remember that, although I have asserted that all "objects" that are *not* properties-as- instantiated are beautiful with respect to some other "objects" (including properties), it has been left open til now whether all beautiful properties are themselves beautiful with respect to other "objects." It will turn out, in fact, that some beautiful properties are indeed beautiful with respect to some other properties and that some are not.

Let us recall that all beautiful "objects" (including beautiful properties) that *are* beautiful with respect to some other "objects" are usually[8] called (simply) beautiful. That is to say, the standard form of our judgments is *X is beautiful (simpliciter)*. I have argued that, at least with respect to those "objects" that can be beautiful with respect to some other "object," a statement of the form *X is beautiful (simpliciter)* implies one or more statements of the form *X is beautiful with respect to Y*. Now although I claim that there is no beauty in any "object" (not a property) other than its beauty with respect to some other

[8] But not always, as Section 30 will show.

17

"objects," I do not mean that any statement of the form *X is beautiful (simpliciter)* is equivalent in meaning to nothing but one or more statements of the form *X is beautiful with respect to Y*. And thus nothing I've said licenses an inference from any set of statements of the form *X is beautiful with respect to Y* to one of the form *X is beautiful (simpliciter)*. In other words, we cannot conclude that an "object" is beautiful (*simpliciter*) from the fact that it is beautiful with respect to something. Helen may not be beautiful (*simpliciter*) even though *with respect to her complexion* she is beautiful. Likewise, Helen's skin may not be beautiful (*simpliciter*) even though *with respect to its clearness* her skin is beautiful. It is absolutely crucial to grasp this point in order to follow the rest of the discussion.

I reiterate, however, that the above qualification in no way compromises my claim that if a theory can account for all that with respect to which every object is beautiful, there is *no* beauty that escapes the grasp of the theory. Of course, what these two claims jointly imply is that whatever further significance a statement like "Helen's skin is beautiful (*simpliciter*)" may have over and above the statements describing that with respect to which Helen's skin is beautiful, it cannot consist, even partially, in pointing out any *additional* beauty in the world. I will not in this essay venture to say what that further significance might be, or even whether there is any further significance. My reason is that I am presenting here a general theory of beauty, not a general theory of statements in which the term "beautiful" and its cognates appear.[9]

---

[9] Having alerted the reader to the distinction between judging that an object is beautiful (*simpliciter*) and judging that it is beautiful with respect to something else, I shall not, most of the time, use the term "(*simpliciter*)." From now on, any use of "beautiful" without a qualifying phrase should be understood as "beautiful (*simpliciter*)."

6. *Experiences of Beauty*

There are some facts about our experiences of beauty reflection on which ultimately led me to the theory I'm about to present. I don't know why these facts helped generate the theory; it is certainly not because I am able to use them to construct an argument for the theory. But I strongly feel, though I cannot show, that they are intimately connected to the theory, and in a way not peculiar to me. I describe them now hoping that others, being reminded of these experiences, will also find them illuminating. These experiences are not, I should add, new discoveries; they have been recognized, under one description or another, for millennia.

We don't, generally speaking, simply see, hear, feel, taste, or otherwise apprehend beauty. Beauty is typically an attention-getter; we suddenly notice it; it breaks into our consciousness. Moreover, it does so gratuitously; it does so despite the fact that we may not have been looking for it, despite the fact that we had no inkling it was going to be there. The beauty of the freeway interchange that we have never seen before suddenly dawns on us as we drive through it. The exotic face of a stranger in the crowd "leaps out" at us as we push our way along in our usual everyday daze. But even beauties we have seen many times before can catch our notice. We anticipate the majestic view as we round the bend, and, as always, it grabs our attention as it comes in sight.

In these situations beauty always appears the "aggressor." The metaphors we use to describe the experiences all point to this fact. Beauty "catches" our attention; it "breaks on us"; it "leaps out" at us; it "strikes" us. We seem powerless before its pull. It seems as if it is not we who give our attention to beauty, but beauty that, as it were, forces our attention on it. Thus we often sensibly recoil when we notice beauty; our head draws back, or feels as if it does.

This "impact" that beauty has on us is not merely emotional. It may be true that "my heart leaps up when I behold the rainbow in the sky," but so do my eyes "light up." The element that I want particularly to stress in our reaction to beauty is its effect on our senses, our perceptual faculties, our minds. Specifically, this effect is one of "expansion." Our eyes are "filled" with the beauty of the landscape, our ears with the sweetness of the melody, our mind with the elegance of the argument. It is as though the receptive faculty were growing larger to take in the abundance offered it. Visual beauty, especially, is like a light dawning on us, flowing out from its source and filling the world and us with itself. Medieval philosophers were sufficiently impressed by this phenomenon to insist that beauty is, in part, *claritas*, which has been aptly translated as "radiance."[10]

Finally, beauty has a tremendous holding power for us. When we perceive a beautiful thing, we don't want to let it go, we never want to stop perceiving it. It is as if our eyes wanted to drown in the sight, our ears in the sound. When the beautiful thing has disappeared, or we have gone our way, we sense a loss, we feel let down. The structure of this feeling is remarkably like post-coital "melancholy." It is no wonder that Plato thought of beauty as seductive and described our relation to it as "love."

Describing the experience of beauty can be as seductive as beauty itself; and, as with all things seductive, there is

[10] For more historical information on this suggestive concept, see Wladyslaw Tatarkiewicz, *History of Aesthetics*, II, ed. C. Barrett (The Hague: Mouton, 1970), 30 and *passim*.

always the risk of losing control. We proceed, then, to the argument.

7. Vividness and the Beauty of Color

I will first work out a theory of beauty of color and later generalize the results to other properties. Eventually I will clarify the reasons for this strategy.

Imagine examples of the following kinds of things that you judge to be beautiful with respect to their color:

- a) an orange cat,
- b) a new red car,
- c) green coastal hills of Southern California in February,
- d) golden coastal hills of Southern California in June,
- e) an orange sunset,
- f) blue sky on a brilliant autumn day.

Now imagine conditions of the following descriptions. A rule for imagining correctly is that you must imagine the conditions as destroying, damaging, or diminishing (whether temporarily or permanently) the beauty of color imagined before.

- a′) The cat comes in from a rainstorm spattered with mud and with grease from a car it has been hiding under.
- b′) The car is two years old, has never been polished, and has been allowed to stand in the sun and rain.
- c′) The rainy season is over, and the hot sun has begun to yellow the grass here and there.
- d′) It is November; the rains have started, and the weeds of the fields have not only been bleached out by the summer sun but have begun to get those tiny, gray specks of decay.

21

e′) The sun is sinking, and the color is getting weaker.

f′) The weather has turned colder, a breeze has come up and blown a light veil of clouds over the sky. The sky remains blue but has a whitish cast to it.

So far we have imagined each of a series of things under two kinds of condition. Under one sort of condition the things are beautiful with respect to the colors, respectively, orange, red, green, golden, orange, and blue. Under the other sort of condition the things are no longer beautiful, or as beautiful, with respect to *those same colors*.[11] Notice, though, that it is, by hypothesis, still true of those things under the second sort of condition that they indeed have the same color as under the first sort. This does not imply that they do *not* have *different* colors under the changed conditions. It merely implies that they are still, respectively, orange, red, green, golden, orange, and blue.

Nevertheless, under conditions (a′) through (f′) something does change in (a) through (f), and change specifically with respect to the colors that make (a) through (f) beautiful. The orange color of the cat becomes dingy and dull; the red of the car becomes faded; the green of the hills becomes pale and splotchy; the gold of the hills becomes bleached and dim; the orange of the sunset becomes faint and pale; the blue of the sky becomes insipid and washed out. There is a natural and straightforward way to generalize from these facts: the beautiful colors, in becoming less vivid, become less beautiful or even

[11] I stress this phrase because they might, under the second condition, yet be beautiful with respect to color, but with respect to some other color, for example, sea green in (c′), or oatmeal in case (d′), or bronze in (e′). I shall have more to say about this point later. They might, of course, also still (under the second kind of condition) be beautiful with respect to some properties other than color properties. But that is irrelevant to the present point.

not beautiful. Vividness is thus an important respect in which color can be beautiful.

The first thing to notice about vividness is that it is a property of degree. One instance of color may be more or less vivid than another instance of color. Now since it is the case that the less vivid an instance of color is the less beautiful it is, then the more vivid an instance of color is, the more beautiful it is, at least with respect to the property of vividness. From this generalization it does not *follow* that a very high degree of vividness in the color of a thing is sufficient to make the color of that thing beautiful with respect to vividness. But the latter is, nevertheless, a reasonable hypothesis. The hypothesis is, moreover, plausible with respect to the beautiful things imagined earlier. An orange cat is beautiful with respect to its color, generally speaking, when the color of its coat is especially vibrant, when it is "more orange" than most cats of that color.[12] The color on a new car just picked up at the dealer's is more vivid than it will ever be again, as vivid as cars with that paint ever are. In cases (c) and (d) I deliberately picked the months of February and June because the hills are, in the normal year at least, never more intensely green and gold, respectively, than in those months. And the blue sky in the early fall, on a clear day, is often "bluer" than at other times because there is generally less moisture in the air and because autumn foliage is likely to intensify the blue by complementing it.

Thus a thing may be beautiful with respect to its color, and the color of the thing may be beautiful with respect to its vividness. Furthermore, it appears that if the color of a thing has a very high degree of vividness, it is beautiful with respect

[12] This does not mean, for reasons I'll discuss later, that a cat whose coat had been sprayed with fluorescent orange paint would be extremely beautiful.

to the property of vividness and, conversely, that if the color of a thing is beautiful with respect to its vividness, then it is vivid to a very high degree. At this stage of the argument the latter claim is only plausible. In the next few sections I will try to substantiate it by exploring the notion of "vividness" as it applies to color. One should keep in mind from the very beginning, though, that I am *not* claiming either (1) that if the color of a thing is beautiful (*simpliciter*), then it is extremely vivid or (2) that if the color of a thing is extremely vivid, then it (the color) is beautiful (*simpliciter*). The claim concerns color only insofar as it is beautiful with respect to vividness. Part of my strategy, though, will be to show that beauty of color is quite frequently nothing but a very high degree of vividness of color. For I ultimately want to argue that, just as the beauty of "objects" that are not properties is nothing but the beauty of properties of those "objects," so the beauty of properties, of which beauty of color is an important subspecies, is reducible to the beauty of properties of degree like vividness.

8. *The Relativity of Vividness*

"Vividness" denotes a scale with respect to which instances of color can be ordered as more or less vivid. There are three ways of using a vividness scale. First, there is a vividness scale relative to each distinct color. One instance of violet, say, can be more or less vivid than another. We can call this kind of vividness "color-relative vividness." Second, one instance of violet may be more color-relatively vivid than an instance of orange and may be said to be more vivid on that account. This we can call "cross-color vividness." Third, the color orange is generally more vivid than the color violet; that is to say, roughly, that most instances of orange are more vivid than most instances of violet, "vivid" meaning here something like "bright" but neither "color-relatively vivid" nor "cross-color vivid." We can call this sort of vividness "absolute vividness." We want now to test the theory that beauty of color can be a very high degree of vividness. Since a very high degree of cross-color vividness in the color of a thing is a special case of a high degree of color-relative vividness in the color of the thing, we need test the theory only with respect to color-relative vividness and absolute vividness.

In the color spectrum, refracted by a prism and reflected on a smooth white surface near the prism, we see the "spectral colors"—red, orange, yellow, green, blue, violet—more vividly than we usually ever see them. It is a consequence of my theory that such instances of color are beautiful with respect to (color-relative) vividness. I don't think this is a seriously disputable consequence. Can anyone look at the colors in such circumstances and not be fascinated by their beauty? Or, if one is now too jaded, can anyone honestly deny that the first time he ever saw the color spectrum like this, his eyes were struck and held by their beauty? Such a spectrum seems to me to be paradigmatically beautiful and offers the purest form of beauty of color. It is the epitome of the medievals' "radiance."

Notice, though, that while the colors as seen in such a spectrum are all at the very highest degree of color-relative vividness, they may still be ranked with respect to absolute vividness, with violet at the bottom and yellow at the top. It is a consequence of my theory that, with respect to absolute vividness, the yellow is more beautiful than the violet. From this, however, it does not follow that the yellow band is more beautiful (*simpliciter*) than the violet band. For one may find, as I

25

do, that the violet band is beautiful with respect to its smoldering, mysterious qualities, which the yellow does not have,
being such an "open" and "naive" color. In fact, I find that
I simply cannot choose the most beautiful of the spectral
bands, for they each have some special qualities that make
them beautiful, in addition to their (color-relative) vividness.

Because of the ambiguity of "vividness," then, an instance
of color may be both beautiful and not beautiful with respect
to vividness. But even if we consider only color-relative vividness, we find that an instance of color may be both beautiful
and not-beautiful with respect to vividness. The reason for
this paradox is one of the most interesting facts about the
beauty of color and one of the most important steps in sub-
stantiating my theory.

Sunsets fade fast. Most of us have no doubt had the experience of seeing a flaming (that is, extremely vivid) orange
sunset, being struck by its beauty, and calling someone to
share the sight only to have her appear after the color has
waned to a ghost of its previous brilliance. The usual reaction
is to say that she's missed the beauty, and that is, of course,
correct insofar as the beauty that we had in mind is the extremely vivid orange color. But the late arrival may not be
disappointed at all, as she exclaims over the beautiful glowing
bronze-gold of the western sky. Having missed the vivid orange,
she sees the very vivid bronze-gold, and hence *a* beauty of the
sunset. And as the reddish tint gradually fades even more from
the sky, a second latecomer may arrive and exclaim—and even
get us and the first late arrival to exclaim—over the lovely *old
gold* of the sky.

What makes this situation possible is that each of the three
persons coming on the scene can actually see extreme vividness
of color in the sunset. Part of the reason is that the sunset

actually changes color, of course. But more significant is the fact that, even at a given instant, the sunset may be more than one color, not in different parts of the sky, but *in the same place*. When the second person sees the sky, it is both a pale (and not very beautiful) orange and a very vivid (and beautiful) bronze-gold. When the third person sees the sky, it is a wan bronze-gold and a vivid old gold.

This fact by no means implies the false proposition that pale orange and vivid bronze-gold, or wan bronze-gold and vivid old gold, are the same color. It does not even imply that *in some cases* these are the same color. The myth that anything colored uniformly all over can and must have only one color stems from a persistent confusion between color and paint or dye. The confusion prevails even with respect to things like sunsets, which are neither painted nor dyed. If I dye all of a piece of white muslin with Rit #74 so that it is uniformly dyed, then it indeed has only one "color" (that is, dye-type) in it, but it may have many colors, even though it is not multicolored. It may, for example, be green, forest green, fir green, dark green. If I put Pittsburgh #W730 all over my wall, the wall may have only one "color" (that is, paint-type) on it, but it has many colors: rosy orange, ice cream orange, hot peach, cantaloupe, etc. And notice that if I put two "colors" (paint-types), say a yellow and a blue, on my wall but mix them together thoroughly first and paint the wall uniformly with the mixture, the wall still may have many colors: green, apple green, lime green, chartreuse, banana green, etc. But the many colors it has will not include yellow and blue.

Now the reason orange and bronze-gold, or bronze-gold and old gold, are not the same color and must be counted as two is that it is false that everything that is one of these colors is necessarily the other, and vice versa. Even when we prefix

the vividness modifiers "pale," "wan," "flaming," "bright,"
or "vivid" itself to the above-mentioned colors, it is not likely
that any of them are coextensive. We can explain the fact that
a thing that is uniformly colored is at once two or more different colors by saying that its color (read as "coloredness")
instantiates two or more different colors. Described in such
a way, the phenomenon of having many colors without being
multicolored is no more puzzling than the fact that a given
plant can be both a bush and tree or that a piece of furniture
can be both a table and a desk. Of course, nothing I have said
about colors should suggest (because it is false) that a uniformly colored thing can be both orange and blue or both red
and green. But neither is it the case that the above bush-tree,
or any other bush, can be both a bush and a skyscraper or that
the above desk-table, or any other desk, can be both a desk
and a river.

The fact that a colored thing that is not multicolored always
has many colors helps explain how colored things can be
beautiful with respect to their extremely vivid colors. Imagine,
for example, a beautiful specimen of Colorado blue spruce,
one that is beautiful because of the extreme vividness of its
color. The tree will be, of course, both green and blue—an
off-blue, a kind of dusty, pale, neutral blue, and a dull, grayish
green. How, then, can it be *vividly* colored? It clearly is not a
vivid green or a vivid blue, and hence it is not beautiful with
respect to these colors. But it is a very vivid Colorado-blue-
spruce-blue. Similarly, there can be beautiful blue clay, beautiful because of the vividness of its color. Yet with respect to
the color blue even the most vividly colored clay is dark and
gray-looking. It is only with respect to the color *clay-blue* that
a chunk of clay can be vivid in color.

Consider one more example. On a walk on a brilliant clear

day in Southern California you suddenly exclaim how beautiful the tile roofs are; you've never seen them as brilliantly red. But your companion is so situated that his view of the roof includes a huge, profusely blossoming cape honeysuckle vine. He is not impressed by the roofs and says they are a drab and muddy orange. Both of your reactions may be justified. With respect to the color *orange* the cape honeysuckle blossoms in the sunlight are incomparably more vivid than any tile roof. The juxtaposition of the two shades of orange forced, as it were, your companion to judge the roof with respect to the color *orange*. You, on the other hand, are perfectly right, for the beauty of the roofs does consist in their beautiful *tile-red* color and their vividness with respect to *that* color.

9. *The Multiplicity of Colors*

One thing that all of the foregoing assumes about colors is that there are more of them than the six on the standard color wheel. I don't think there is any absolutely precise general way of determining what colors there are, but some indicators do exist. In addition to the colors signified by the obvious one-word color terms in English, there are colors corresponding to hyphenated compounds of such terms, such as greenish-yellow, red-violet, purplish-blue. There are also color terms made by joining a "character" term, whether metaphorical or not, to any of the preceding types of terms: "hot pink," "deep blue," "dark green," "true red." Then there are the descriptions made in terms of the first two kinds of color terms plus the name of a sort of thing: "cherry red," "lemon yellow," "sea green." The latter phrases mean, respectively, "red character-istic of cherries," "yellow characteristic of lemons," and "green

29

characteristic of seas." Thus most color terms that have or can be construed in the form "*F* characteristic of *X*" also each designate a distinct color. Sometimes primary color terms are joined with proper names to form terms for distinct colors, as in Chinese red or French blue. In general, all terms of the sort mentioned in this paragraph can be taken as each designating a distinct color.

But the last sentence is only generally, not strictly, true. First we must allow for the possibility that some of the above sorts of terms are synonymous with others. Moreover, sometimes firms that manufacture colored items will attach color names to them that have no descriptive content, but are given merely to surround the item with an aura of excitement or importance, such as "Eleanor (Roosevelt) blue" for clothing or "Acapulco red" for lipstick. Such artificial terms may eventually come to stand for distinct color concepts, but when they are first introduced, they can be glossed only as "the blue of *these* clothes" or "the red of *this* lipstick." The reason that terms like the last two cannot function to designate a distinct color is that, generally, color descriptions that relate whatever is described by them by means of "like" or its synonyms to definite and particular colored things cannot function to designate a distinct color. I have in mind descriptions like "the color of my raincoat," "the color of the Empress Eugenie's favorite dress," and "the color of the glass of the Seagram Building." And the reason that the latter terms fail to designate a distinct color is that we can still ask, having been given these descriptions, what color *that* is; and, furthermore, we can still get more than one answer in color terms that do not refer to definite particular things. We should also except from the above generalization all descriptions of color made up of one of a previously listed type of description coupled with a term that designates, explicitly or implicitly, some degree of vivid-ness. Thus words like "dull," "drab," "pale," "bright," "burning," "brilliant," "lively," "dusty," "radiant," "muddy," attached to color terms should not be taken as further specifying the color described by the phrase following it. Apart from these kinds of exceptions, though, we can think of there being a different color for each distinct color description.

It begins to look as if there may be no instance of color that is not vivid relative to *some* color that it is. For it seems to be the case that even unvivid instances of, say, blue can be at the same time instances of other colors—ice blue, slate blue, smokey blue, ultramarine blue, powder blue, plum blue, ember blue, or baby blue—relative to which they may be vivid. What this means, in part, is that beauty with respect to vividness of color is more widespread than we might initially suppose. And this fact, in itself, is a strength, not a weakness, of the proposition I am arguing, namely, that very, very often beauty of color is reducible to beauty with respect to vividness. For it is a fact (1) that many different shades and tints of a given hue can be beautiful, and (2) that experiences of color beauties of relatively obscure and subtle kinds are communicated precisely by point-ing out previously unnoticed shades or tints in the color of a thing.

In any case, even supposing that every instance of color were an extremely vivid case of some color or other, it would not at all follow that every instance of color is beautiful (*simpliciter*). The reason is that there are more properties that an instance of color can have besides vividness—for example, harshness or garishness. Thus a piece of fluorescent orange plastic discovered on a nature walk in the desert may be vividly colored. Yet in that environment, with its subtle and neutral coloration, the vivid orange may well appear harsh and garish. And the harsh-

31

ness and garishness may, in that context, outweigh the vividness so that the instance of orange color is ugly and not
beautiful. The distinction we must keep in mind here is the
difference between the instance of color C and the vividness of
that instance. It may be that the instance of C is beautiful (*simpliciter*) and beautiful with respect to vividness, that is, because it
is an extremely vivid instance of C. But it might also be that there
is some beauty in an instance of C by virtue of its extreme
vividness, while C in this same instance, because of some other
of its properties, is not beautiful (*simpliciter*).

10. *Vividness and the Context of Color*

Despite the plethora of colors, not every instance of color is
vivid relative to some color for the good reason that vividness
in an instance of color is not dependent only on color param-
eters like hue and saturation. The vividness of a thing's color
also depends upon the environment of that thing. Since Plato's
time people have known that what is beautiful is not always,
and under all conditions, beautiful. This is strikingly so with
respect to beauty of color. A flower that is gorgeous in the sunlight is nothing special on a gray day. Or a tie that is ugly and
drab when worn against one shirt is eye-catching with another.
The color in a painting that is uninteresting when seen from
a distance of forty feet becomes luminously beautiful when
viewed up close. These commonplace facts are explainable in
terms of the theory that one important feature of colors that
makes them beautiful is their extreme vividness. For vividness,
too, varies with respect to these sorts of context.

Why is a beautiful day a clear, sunny day? A large part of the
reason is that every color is more vivid in sunlight. Not all

lighting, of course, has the effect of making color more vivid. If the light has a color of its own, as does most artificial light, it *can* change the color beyond recognition. Furthermore, if there is too much light on a color, the color can be obscured by the lighting by being blanked out. Color may be obscured simply because the colored surface is too shiny, for bright highlights prevent us from seeing the color. The latter phenomenon suggests another condition of vividness in a color. Vividness may depend simply on the angle from which a color is viewed. If the light on a color is *in your eyes*, the color may be whited out. But if you change your position so that the light source is focussed on the color but hidden from you, the color may appear luminous and hence quite beautiful.

The degree of vividness, and hence at least some of the beauty, of a color will often change depending upon the surrounding colors. Anyone who has tried to put together fabrics with complex color schemes—like ties and shirts—knows this to be so. You try to find a shirt that not only will match the red in the tie but will not drab out the yellow stripe. If you're successful, you will finally put the tie against a shirt and the yellow stripe will "light up." In the common idiom, the shirt "brings out" the yellow in the tie, which simply means that it makes the yellow in the tie more vivid. There is probably no absolutely general way of accounting for the phenomenon of "bringing out" a color, but there are a couple of well-known principles. If the color of a thing is surrounded by tints or shades of the same color, it will appear more vivid. The reason for this is obvious: a tint of a color is paler, and a shade is drabber, so the color in its "pure" form is highlighted. Also, if a color is surrounded by complementary colors, it will generally appear more vivid. This phenomenon is apparently connected with the fact that after-images of a color are in the complementary color.

Naturally, not every environment of a color consisting of its complement will make the color more vivid. A brilliant yellow expanse can completely "drown" a small blue spot from a distance of more than four or five feet. Thus the same spot, when viewed from a distance of twelve inches, may be very vivid, whereas from a distance of twelve feet it may be merely a nondescript "hole" in an overpoweringly vivid yellow field. In this case vividness or the lack of it depends upon distance from the viewer. This sort of condition, of course, can increase or decrease the vividness of a color even when it is not surrounded by its complement. Thus the orange plastic in the desert, mentioned a few pages back, may appear quite vivid, and not even garish, when seen very close-up, when it "fills" the eyes of the viewer and permits no comparison between it and its surroundings. But, when viewed from a considerable distance, it may have little or no color-character and appear only as a small "disturbance" in the subtly colored landscape. It is when viewed from a middle distance that the vivid orange of the plastic appears also to be garish. A similar effect can occur even when complementary colors, which "in themselves" are extremely vivid and therefore beautiful, are juxtaposed so that they in effect "compete" with one another and become thereby "noisy" and garish. These properties may in turn make the colors unbeautiful despite the fact that some beauty—namely, that with respect to their extreme vividness—is present in them both.

11. *Vividness and Appearance*

In the preceding two sections I have argued that the vividness of a color of a thing depends upon contextual factors. I have not tried to give a comprehensive theory of the contextual conditions of vividness. I pointed out only some of the important kinds of context that condition vividness: the quality and quantity of light on the color, the color surroundings of a color, and the position of an observer with respect to the color.

It may look at this point as if vividness of color, however closely related to beauty of color, is only a matter of how color *appears* under certain conditions. Thus it is true to say that in sunlight any color appears more vivid than under clouds, that a yellow spot will appear more vivid surrounded by a field of baby blue, and that the orange plastic appears more vivid when seen up close. So if one kind of beauty of color is extreme vividness of color, colors can *appear* more beautiful under some conditions than under others.

The latter consequence of my theory, of course, is one we should expect. For nearly everything, including colors, does appear more beautiful under certain conditions and less so under others. This fact has also been known since at least as far back as Plato's time. But the fact has been construed to mean that beauty is a matter of the appearance of things. Insofar as such a construal is a mere restatement of the fact noted above, I have no quarrel with it. Sometimes, however, the construal holds that beauty concerns *merely* the appearances of things and *not* their reality. That, however, is false.

Sometimes "appears" and its cognates and synonyms are used to make a contrast with what is real or what is the case. Thus under certain conditions a short man may appear tall: when he is in the midst of dwarfs or children, when he is viewed from the floor two feet in front of him, or when he is wearing lifts and a hat. Likewise, an older man may appear to be younger when he is in a dim light, when he is viewed from a distance, or when he is dressed in clothes typically worn by younger men. In both these situations the appearances are contrary to the reality, so that it would be false to say that the

35

man *is* tall, or *is* younger, under the described conditions. "Appearance" terms used with respect to vividness and also with respect to beauty do not always have the import they have in the preceding examples. Colors not only generally *appear* but *are* more vivid and hence, usually, more beautiful in the sun than in the gloom. Vivid colors *are* as well as *appear* more vivid when seen up close or when they are next to the "right" color. In other words, with respect to vividness and beauty, the "is" and "appear" vocabularies are not always contrastive, but are sometimes interchangeable. There is nothing unusual about this fact, that is, nothing that is unique to vividness. As I will argue later, a similar interchangeability between "is" and "appear" vocabularies obtains with respect to many, if not most, beautiful properties.

I should note here, though, that nothing I have said in this section about "being" and "appearing" pertains to yet another problem about "being" and "appearing" with respect to vividness and beauty. It is sometimes claimed about aesthetic properties that they admit of no contrast between *really being* attributable to a "thing" and *only appearing* attributable. As I will illustrate later, I do believe that the "aesthetic property" of beauty does admit of this contrast. That is to say, we can mistakenly perceive a thing to be beautiful or not beautiful. The sense of "appearing" I discuss above in this section is not related to the mistaken perception of beauty, but only to the context-bound nature of beauty.

12. *Other Beauties of Color*

So far I have argued that often, when the color of a thing is beautiful, it is beautiful because of its vividness, and that if the color is very vivid, it is likely, but not necessarily, beautiful (*simpliciter*). Not all color that is beautiful, however, is so because of its vividness. The cloud touched ever so lightly by the setting sun may be just barely rose-tinged. The cloud may still be beautiful, but beautiful not because of the vividness of the rose color. It might be the *delicacy* of the color in this context that provides the beauty. A dark blue fabric may be beautiful because of the *depth* of the color. An off-green color, grayish and yellowish at once, may be beautiful because of its *sultriness*, and an orange color may be beautiful precisely because of the *earthiness* that places it on the drab end of the vividness scale relative to the color orange.

Properties other than vividness are especially important in locating the beauties of those "colors" that contain little or no hue—the so-called neutrals: black, brown, gray, and white. "Vividness" does not properly apply to these colors. Instead, there are other properties, like the richness of a brown, the depth or intensity of a black, the purity or brilliance of a white, that make them beautiful.

It may occur to some that the sorts of color property listed above are not really properties of *color*, because it is frequently due to noncolor properties of the colored "things" that the above properties are applied. Thus the depth of a blue in a fabric may depend upon the fact that the fabric is velvet and not gabardine. Likewise, the rose tinge on the cloud may seem delicate because it is on a cloud and not on an automobile. Similarly, the depth of the blackness on a cloudless and moonless night against which we see the stars is surely a function of the fact that it is limitless space and not the inside of a gigantic glass bowl that we see. These undeniable facts, however, do not imply that the respective properties are not properties of *color*. For the case is not essentially different with respect to vividness, which is undeniably a property of color in a thing. As pointed out earlier, the vividness of color in a thing may depend upon a number of features of a thing other than its color. It is also true, though not mentioned before, that vividness of color will vary depending upon the surface, texture, and consistency of the colored thing. A color on silk is usually going to be more vivid than the "same" color on wool. Red vinyl is generally more vivid than red leather.

The properties other than vividness that can make colors beautiful may be unlimited; there may be no way to list them all. But there would be no point in listing them all in any case. For they all share with vividness a crucial feature; they are all properties of degree. Just as the color in a thing can be more or less vivid, color can be more or less deep, delicate, mysterious, bold, earthy, sultry, smoldering, fresh, naive, subtle, brilliant, or rich. And with respect to every one of these properties, if the color in a thing has the property to a very high degree, there is beauty in the color with respect to that property. I offer no specific arguments for the last proposition but leave it to the reader's own experience for confirmation. Note, however, that in that proposition I claim only that, with a high degree of a property of color, there is beauty *in the color*. I do not claim either that the color of the thing is thereby beautiful (*simpliciter*) or that the thing is thereby beautiful (*simpliciter*). Having beauty in a thing's color *may*, and may *often*, make the color as well as the thing beautiful (*simpliciter*). But that there is beauty with respect to any of the properties that apply to color in a thing —that is, that the color has a high degree of that property—does not entail that the color is beautiful or that the thing is beautiful. More discussion of this point will come later.

38

13. *Properties of Qualitative Degree*

Thus far we have one element of a theory of beautiful color, namely, that if the color of a thing is beautiful, it possesses at least one property in a very high degree. I am ready now to formulate a general theory of beauty. In order to do so, however, I must clarify a key concept in that theory, the notion of a "property of qualitative degree" (henceforth PQD). All the properties with respect to which the color of a thing may be beautiful are PQDs. A generic feature of any PQD *F* is that it be possible for one "object" to be more or less *F* than another "object." A specific feature of any PQD *F* is that the degree to which one "object" is more or less *F* than another is not numerically determinable according to a single scale that can measure the degree to which any given "object," is more or less *F* than any other "object." The generic feature excludes from the class of PQDs such nondegree properties as *being square, being full,* and *being pregnant.* The specific feature excludes such properties of quantitative degree as *being heavy, being hot, being tall,* and *being large.* The specific feature of PQDs, moreover, means that there is no *uniform* and *general* scale of measurement for the degrees of a PQD. Without this feature the distinction between PQDs and properties of quantitative degree cannot be made. The reason is that, given a sufficiently narrowing set of conditions, a numerical degree scale could easily be constructed to measure the difference of degree in which any two "objects" that meet those conditions possess any PQD.

The last point can be illustrated with respect to vividness of color. A bright yellow paint can be used to paint a wooden chip. A unit (however small) of white paint can be mixed with the original yellow and a chip painted with the result. This procedure can be repeated each time adding one more unit of white to the previous mixture of white and yellow down to the final chip, which can be as pale as you please. The chips can then be arranged in the order in which they were produced. Some neighboring chips in this arrangement may not be noticeably different from one another. But a series of chips can be produced such that each chip is just barely noticeably different from each of its neighbors by testing the discrimination responses of a large sampling of percipients, a chip being removed from the original series if a statistically significant portion of the subjects do not perceive it as different from the preceding one. The chips in the resulting series can then be sequentially numbered. Then, for any two chips in the series, it will be possible to determine *by counting chips* how much more or less vivid one is than the other.

Notice, however, that this determination is valid only if the quantity and quality of light falling on each chip is constant and only when a constant distance between chips and observer is maintained. Furthermore, there are other conditions built into the scale itself. First, it is a scale only for measuring vividness of the variety of yellow that all of those chips, and only those, instantiate. It therefore does not measure vividness with respect to any other color, not even yellow colors of which a "more vivid" chip than the top chip might mark the highest degree of vividness. Second, all the chips are made of a single kind of surface and substance—painted wood. Third, the scale can measure lack of vividness with respect only to *tints* of the top-chip yellow and only tints resulting from mixture of a certain white. The resulting scale of measuring vividness, though numerical, is by no means general. As far as I know, moreover, even though there are many complex ways of measuring color differences, none of these standard scales is equipped to measure them with respect to *all* of the variables upon which vividness of color depends. Furthermore, since these variables intersect in complex ways, there seems to be no hope of devising a single, numerical vividness scale short of reproducing in the scale every discriminably different instance of a color. And even then we would have a vividness scale for only *one* color and would need similar ones for each of the indefinitely large number of colors! Reflection will show that numerical scales like the one imagined above are theoretically possible with respect to any PQD and that they are all equally doomed to have a considerably less than general applicability.

We have then isolated a class of properties, the PQDs. Let me further divide the class of PQDs by distinguishing all those that are deficiencies, lacks, or defects from those that are not. Properties may be deficiencies, lacks, or defects in either of two ways: either universally, or relative to sorts of "objects" to which they apply. *Being blemished, being deformed, being uncouth, being dilapidated, being unhealthy, being silly, being imprecise, being sallow* are examples of the former. Examples of the latter are *being rough* (applied to a skin, or a road, but not to eucalyptus bark), *being shiny* (applied to a gabardine fabric, but not to an automobile finish), *being fat* (applied to adults, but not to babies), *being smooth* (applied to tire treads, but not to roads), *being sad* (applied to days, but not to music and not necessarily to people).

One more division is necessary. We shall also want to distinguish those properties that signify the *appearance* of lack, deficiency, or defect from those properties that signify neither lacks, deficiencies, nor defects nor their appearance. I have in mind here such properties as *being unhealthy-looking, being sallow-looking, being rotten-smelling, being putrid-tasting, being evil-*

41

looking. The latter sort of properties, like properties of lack, deficiency, or defect, may also be either "universal" or "relative."

14. *The New Theory of Beauty Stated*

In Section 5 I concluded that a perfectly comprehensive theory of beauty could be a theory of the beauty of properties because there is no beauty in "objects" that is not beauty with respect to one or more properties of the "objects." The analysis of beauty in color allows us to think that even the beauty of some "beautiful properties," like color properties, can be further reduced. For we can say that there is no beauty of color that is not beauty with respect to one or more PQDs. Generalizing from beauty of color, then, we can say that a perfectly comprehensive theory of beauty can be a theory of beautiful PQDs.

Before stating the theory, however, I must make one important delimitation of the notion of a PQD. As thus far delimited, the class of PQDs includes whatever is signified by "beautiful." But since we have determined that the subject matter of a theory of beauty is located by the class of beautiful PQDs, we do not want beauty to be both the analysans and the analysand. We must, therefore, exclude beauty and all of its synonyms, whatever they may turn out to be in particular, from the class of PQDs. What this restriction will amount to is that any adjective or adjectival phrase that can be modified by "more" or "less," where these terms are taken in the qualitative sense explained earlier, will *not* count as signifying a PQD if what is so signified can, like beauty, be construed as a way *of being F.* And we will take the following as the formal *mark* of the possibility of such a construction: the adjective (or adjectival phrase) cannot be placed, without creating a redundancy, in the blank of sentences of the form "*X is beautifully* ___." This

42

test will exclude from the class of PQDs *beauty, gorgeousness, exquisiteness,* as well as (some of the time) *brilliance, radiance,* and others.

Most succinctly expressed, then, the New Theory of Beauty I am putting forth is: *A PQD of an "object" is beautiful if and only if (1) it is not a property of deficiency, lack, or defect, (2) it is not a property of the "appearance" of deficiency, lack, or defect, and (3) it is present in that "object" in a very high degree; and any "object" that is not a PQD is beautiful only if its possesses, proximately or ultimately,*[13] *at least one PQD present in that "object" to a very high degree.*

Note that the New Theory specifies only a necessary, not a sufficient, condition for an "object" that is not a PQD to be beautiful. Thus I am explicitly distinguishing between a comprehensive theory of beauty and a theory that lays down necessary *and sufficient* conditions for the proper application of the predicate "beautiful" and all of its cognates and synonyms. This is to say again that the theory takes as its subject matter only beauty, not all of the utterances in which "beauty" and its synonyms and cognates are used.

15. *The Argument Strategy*

The strategy of my argument in support of the New Theory has already been launched and shall be continued in the following sections. I want here to describe and partially defend that strategy. I want also to specify exactly what it would take to disconfirm the New Theory (henceforth NTB).

[13] An "object" possesses a PQD *proximately* if, when the question-procedure described earlier is applied, the first result is that PQD. An "object" possesses a PQD *ultimately* if the question-procedure must be applied more than once to yield that PQD.

As I indicated earlier, I believe it is impossible to find a theory that specifies necessary *and sufficient* conditions for any "object" to be beautiful. The failure thus far of all attempts to produce a general theory of beauty is due, I think, to failure to recognize that fact and to failure to see that such is not the only route to a general theory of beauty. These beliefs of mine are speculative, and I offer no arguments for them. They can be shown false by the discovery of a set of necessary and sufficient conditions for any "object" to be beautiful. I have argued, however, that the beauty of any "object" that is not a property is always in principle ultimately specifiable in terms of at least one "beautiful property." And I have, on the basis of an analysis of the beauty of one class of properties, namely, color properties, asserted that the beauty of any property that is not a PQD is specifiable in terms of at least one PQD. I have concluded, then, that a theory giving necessary and sufficient conditions for the beauty of PQDs is a perfectly general theory of beauty. In other words, even if NTB does not provide sufficient, but only necessary, conditions for the application of "beautiful" (*sans phrase*) to all "objects," there is nevertheless no beauty that escapes the grasp of the Theory.

I introduced NTB by a discussion of color because I think beauty of color is less esoteric than most beauty and therefore less subject to extreme disagreements. Moreover, because color is a relatively restricted realm with respect to the sorts of properties that make it beautiful, it seemed safer to come to the crucial generalization about the high degree of PQDs from within the realm of color. But it is also because the applicability of NTB to color can be seen only when (a) the multiplicity of colors and (b) the color-relativity of vividness are accepted, and because these points need detailed argument to seem plausible, that I chose beauty of color to introduce NTB.

The New Theory, of course, goes far beyond the realm of color. And it can be disconfirmed by discovering (a) one or more beautiful "objects" that are not PQDs and that are beautiful but not with respect to one or more PQDs, or (b) one or more "objects" that possess an extremely high degree of one or more PQDs (which are not properties of lack, defect, or deficiency) but that are not beautiful with respect to those PQDs.

In what follows I will, first, illustrate NTB with a variety of examples of visual and aural beauty, both in nature and in art, making points analogous to those made with respect to vividness. Second, I will argue by means of examples for the applicability of NTB to tastes, smells, and feelings. Third, I will show how NTB accounts for utilitarian, intellectual, and moral beauty. Fourth, I will show how on the basis of NTB disagreements about what is beautiful are explicable and why beauty is currently neither a useful nor a widely used term in critical discourse about the arts. Fifth, I will demonstrate the relevance of NTB to the traditional notion of "beauty as harmony." Throughout all of these discussions I shall be implicitly showing how many ideas that have persisted for millennia in a variety of forms in the history of speculations about beauty can be accommodated by and integrated into NTB. I shall conclude this essay by discussing briefly the objectivity of beauty, as determined by NTB, and then explaining why we enjoy perceiving beauty.

16. *Beauty and the Looks of Things*

The way things look is, aside from color, the most important kind of properties that make for visual beauty. These properties are signified by predicates of the form *F-looking*, although often the hyphenated form is merely implicit in our ordinary use of language. Things can, of course, be F-looking in different degrees, no matter what F is. They are most beautiful with respect to their F-look the more F-looking they are; and their F-look is clearly beautiful if it is present in an extremely high degree. A variety of examples can illustrate this point.

When the sun comes up behind the Santa Ana Mountains, a segment of the ridgeline is especially beautiful, specifically because of a certain craggy, dentated look. An interesting fact is that, although the ridgeline has that look from the plain for the whole day on most days, it is not *beautiful* during the whole day. The reasons are (1) that only when the sun is in the East is the sky so luminous that the craggy look is intensified and (2) that the smog, which obscures the ridgeline later in the day, is rarely present at sunrise. Moreover, farther to the south the ridgeline is less beautiful, even in the early morning, because the craggy look is less pronounced, the ridgeline becoming flatter and more insipid. Now although the craggy look of the local mountains strikes me as beautiful under the described conditions, I know it does so chiefly because the ridgeline at that point not only is very craggy-looking but is the *most* craggy-looking thing around as I drive to work. But I can recall the Dents du Midi south of Lake Geneva, or almost any ridge of the Dolomites, and remember incomparably more beautiful craggy looks there.

The hills nearer the campus are gentler. They are undulating and are covered with grass. They can be very beautiful, and when they are, it is often because they are so sensuous-looking. When the evening sun deepens their shadows and accentuates their curves and brings out their soft, grassy texture, they look as though it would feel delightful to run one's hands, like a god, over the breast-like contours and stroke them. Now the

46

hills lose some of their sensuous look in those places where there are rock outcroppings or where there are patches of chaparral. Although the rocks and chaparral have their own beauty, from a distance they only "roughen" the hills and make them less beautiful than the hills with the more sensuous-looking surface.

Similar phenomena occur in art. One of the properties that distinguishes Giotto's painting is, as Bernard Berenson has taught us, the tactility (tactile look) of his figures, the look they have of being "massy" and palpable. When a scene or a passage in a Giotto fresco is beautiful, it is often so because of the high degree of tactility of the figures. Like most artists, Giotto is not always at his best. Nearly every scene in the Scrovegni Chapel has better and worse figures. And with respect to tactility, as well as other features, the frescoes at Assisi are inferior to those at Padua. In the "Vision of St. Joachim" at Padua, for example, the tactility of the Joachim figure is clearly more beautiful than those of the shepherds. The figure of the nearer shepherd in that scene, however, is by no means ugly. For not only does it show some of Giotto's tactility, but it has, in addition, extraordinarily graceful lines. The figure of Joachim, too, is graceful, but it is its tactility that really stands out, intensified by the compact-ness and immobility of the sleeping figure. In contrast to both of these figures, the one of Christ being baptized, also at Padua, is simply not beautiful at all, at least from the neck down. It is neither tactile nor graceful. Nudes were not Giotto's forte; he usually depended upon enveloping draperies to give the tactile look to his figures. Moreover, because Giotto's knowledge of anatomy was elementary, Christ's body is still, awkward, and misshapen.

Michelangelo's "David" is beautiful, not for its grace, though it is not ungraceful, nor for its fine proportions, which

47

are nearly nonexistent, but for its intense look of energy, a quality made the more intense for being embodied in a stationary being. The energetic look of the work comes not merely from David's piercing gaze and his battle-ready muscles, but also from the force of the sculpturing: the deep cuts to make the heavy-ringleted hair, the sharp crease of the lower eyelids, the definite edges of the lower lip and the wings of the nose, the clean definition of the fingernails, the protuberant nipples. This energetic look is, of course, not unique to the "David"; it is the stamp of Michelangelo. And it is that (but not only that) which gives beauty to much of Michelangelo's work. Yet some of Michelangelo's work lacks this variety of beauty. The four small statues on the Piccolomini Altar in Siena, for instance, have only intimations of this Michelangelesque energy and nothing like the stunning beauty of the "David." The lack is not due to their smaller size. It is precisely that deep and incisive cutting that is missing. For this reason they have always looked unfinished to me, looked like sketches of what they should have been.

17. *The Relativity of Looks*

Properties signified by predicates of the form *F-looking* behave in a way analogous to vividness. Recall that vividness has scales of degree that are relative to each color. Similarly, the degrees of an *F*-look are, in general, relative to the sort of "object" that has the *F*-look. Take, for example, the property of being craggy-looking. I have already discussed this property with respect to mountain ridgelines. But human faces may also be craggy-looking. A man may, in middle age, have a beautiful face, beautiful for the reason that his face is, in a high and exceptional degree, craggy-looking. It will then be rough, angular, sharp, and lean, and having piercing eyes. The face may even be better-looking at age forty-five than at twenty, when its angularity was ill-suited to its freshness and smoothness and to its frank, innocent eyes, and better-looking than at sixty-five when, though still craggy, its mien is softened by collapsing muscles and dimmed eyes. But there is no meaning to the question whether the man's face at forty-five is more craggy-looking than the Dents du Midi on a clear and sunny day. The craggy looks of faces and of mountains are not, on a scale of craggy looks, any more comparable than are their beauties. It is simply meaningless to ask for such a comparison unless, on the analogy to cross-color vividness, we want to know how a face ranks on the scale of craggy-looking faces in comparison to the rank of a mountain ridgeline on the scale of craggy-looking mountains. And, as with comparisons of cross-color vividness, only rather gross comparisons can be made—for example, a very craggy-looking face to a not so craggy-looking ridgeline, or vice versa.

It might be objected that the incomparability of craggy-looking faces and mountains is merely a function of the fact that "craggy" is metaphorical when applied to faces but literal when applied to mountains. Consider, then, the example of *being solid-looking*. The treeless mountains east of here are extremely beautiful on those sunny and smogless days when, in the evening, the sun burns purple shadows into them. It is then that their three-dimensional form comes so alive that one can almost feel their solidity at the tips of one's fingers. The mountains are much more beautiful at such times than they are when the smog obscures their tridimensionality by whitening their shadows and fuzzing the hard, sculptured lines of their ridges. But try to compare the solid look of the hills under these conditions to the Brahmin bull that stands against the sky on the top of the knoll, its blackness contrasting sharply with the fragile, golden pattern of grass and its hump looming up, the biggest thing about it. The bull, too, is beautiful in that setting and beautiful because it is so solid-looking, so intensely three-dimensional. One can, of course, compare the bull to another bull in a depression between two knolls, standing in shadow with its hump obscured, and judge it more beautiful. One can compare the mountains this evening to their appearance this morning or yesterday and find them incomparably more beautiful. But how can one answer the question: "Which is more beautiful, the very solid-looking mountain or the very solid-looking bull?" Because the solid look of each depends upon such different kinds of features, the two beauties are incomparable, even though the beauty of each is traceable to a solid look. But note that this incomparability cannot be laid to a difference in the meaning in each case either of "solid" or of "solid-looking."

Parallel examples of incomparability in the degree of F-lookingness are plentiful in art. Consider only the look of monumental strength in many of Henry Moore's sculptures and the look of monumental strength possessed by the Egyptian pyramids. Is there any sense to the question: "Which have more of a look of strength?" It seems to me not, because there is no way of answering it. Moore makes very strong-looking figures; the Egyptians made very strong-looking pyramids. Insofar as the *beauty* of each sort of thing depends, at least in part, upon its being strong-looking, the beauty of each cannot be compared to the beauty of the other, except in the cross-sortal manner indicated previously. In this case, of course, there is an obvious sense in which any of the Egyptian pyramids *looks* stronger than any of Moore's figures. That is the sense in which the pyramids look as if they could withstand more force directed toward moving or demolishing them. But looking strong is not the same as being strong-looking. To attribute the former to a thing is to express doubt or agnosticism with respect to its strength; to attribute the latter is to say that it has a certain kind of appearance.

Another example of incomparability of degree in art is the buoyant look of a building like, say, Saarinen's TWA Terminal in New York and the buoyant look that a dancer with unusual *ballon* may have. Both buildings and dancers dancing may be beautiful partly because of their buoyant looks, but it makes little sense to ask of a given buoyant-looking building whether it is more or less buoyant than Nureyev in last night's performance. Still, as with other sort-relative properties, there is a sense in which it is meaningful to compare buoyant buildings and buoyant dancers. We can agree perhaps that dancers dancing are *generally* more buoyant-looking than buildings. This statement means something like "More dancers are buoyant-looking (for dancers) than buildings are buoyant-looking (for buildings)."

I can offer no general theory to explain *why* craggy looks, solid looks, buoyant looks, and other beautiful PQDs like them possess different scales of degrees for different ranges of "objects" to which they apply. The reason may lie deep in the nature of such properties. As far as this essay is concerned, though, I only point to this feature as a fact. Its meaning is that the beauty of an "object" with respect to any *F*-look is an extremely high degree of *F*-lookingness *for that sort of "object."* This point is generalizable to all PQDs, and I shall be illustrating that general point from time to time in the exposition that follows. I should note here that I don't pretend to know how "objects" can be collected into *sorts* independently of our

51

intuitions concerning the comparability or incomparability they have vis-à-vis some PQD. It is possible, thus, that a single "object" may belong to different sorts with respect to different PQDs.

18. *Other Varieties of Visual Beauty and Other Varieties of Relativity*

Colors and "looks" are not the only kinds of visual properties that are beautiful. Some, like gracefulness, elegance, and being powerfully built, can be purely visual, although they may also apply to things either heard, like music, or kinaesthetically felt, like dances, or touched, like bodies. I take it that no one disputes either that these are indeed beautiful properties, in my sense, or that possession of them to an *extremely high degree* is specifically what makes for beauty with respect to them. They do, however, illustrate in interesting ways the general principle of relativity adumbrated above.

Figures in Renaissance paintings are frequently beautiful because of their gracefulness. This is true both of Botticelli's three graces in the "Primavera" and of the Virgin and two saints in the "Madonna of the Harpies" by Andrea del Sarto. But it is impossible to answer the question which figures are more graceful, Botticelli's or del Sarto's, even though the comparison requested here is between nothing so different as mountains and faces, or human figures and pyramids. If we try to give some response, we are likely to go back and forth in our estimate: Botticelli's are the more graceful—see the exquisite lines of the bodies, those folds in the gossamer garments, the swirled hair; no, del Sarto's figures are more graceful, for notice how precariously balanced Botticelli's graces are, how artificially posed their limbs are; del Sarto's figures are so balanced, so well-placed; every part of the bodies leads the eye naturally to the other parts along *implicit* lines connecting each of the parts, even those that are obscured by shadows. Note, though, how when we appreciate the gracefulness of the figures, we point to different properties in the Botticelli and the del Sarto: explicit lines in the former, implicit ones created by placement of the body in the latter. This difference shows that although we are talking about the grace of *figures* in both paintings, we are nevertheless talking about different *aspects* of the figures in each. This example is not essentially different, therefore, from the strong looks in the Moore sculpture and in the pyramids. It is the thickness of the bodies and the relative absence of articulation of bodily parts in the Moore figures that yield the strong look there. But in the pyramids it is the wide base, the stark planes, the straight lines, the superhuman scale that provide the look of strength.

The incomparability of gracefulness in Botticelli and del Sarto helps show why beauties in the work of different artists frequently defeat comparison, even when the beauties are ostensibly so much alike—a fact that has been widely noticed but never explained. The incomparability between artists is not perfectly general, however. After all, if Botticelli can paint a less beautifully graceful figure than his best ones, surely other artists can produce less graceful figures than any of Botticelli's graceful ones. And, in fact, they do; but when they do, the gracefulness of their figures depends upon just the same properties of their figures as does the gracefulness in Botticelli's figures. Thus some figures by Raphael, Lorenzo di Credi, da Vinci, the earlier Michelangelo, Titian, and Tintoretto, among others, are comparable to del Sarto's with respect to gracefulness. But the gracefulness of late Gothic madonnas and of Modigliani's ladies are no more comparable to the gracefulness in del Sarto than is the gracefulness in the Botticelli.

For some PQDs there is an even more interesting kind of incomparability than the one we have just observed. There are beautiful properties having applicability over two or more sorts of "objects" that are related in such a way that if the property as applicable to members of one sort is, in some circumstance, also applicable to "objects" of another sort, then it is no longer a beautiful property of those "objects" but is a property of deficiency, lack, or defect. Now let me illustrate this abstract point.

Human beings, like other animals, can be beautiful because they are powerfully built. Most readers have, I presume, well enough negotiated their adolescent identity crises to recognize that being powerfully built is a beautiful property with respect to both men and women.[14] Just as with other of the "incomparable" properties we have been discussing, it is possible to compare the property of being powerfully built *across* the ranges of men and women and say that a (given) woman is more powerfully built than a (given) man, and vice versa. What this statement would mean is that the woman is more powerfully built (for a woman) than the man is (for a man), and vice versa. It is also possible to say, whether it is empirically true or not, that men are generally more powerfully built than are women, when this means that more men are powerfully built (for men) than women are (for women).

Being powerfully built is relative, then, to at least two "sorts" of human beings: male and female. That property functions differently in this respect from the property of *being powerful*. The latter is not only not necessarily relative to male and fe-

[14] Recall that to admit so much is not necessarily to admit that any human being who is powerfully built, and beautifully so, is beautiful.

male sorts, it is not necessarily relative to any subsorts whatever of the general category of "objects" that can, logically,
be powerful. And this fact, in turn, fits together with the fact
that being powerful, unlike being powerfully built, is not a
PQD, but is a property of quantitative degree.[15] Thus it is that
a man who is more *powerfully built* than another may, merely
because of differences in height and weight, be less *powerful*
than the other. Being powerfully built has to do, not with the
amount of brute strength a person can muster, but with the
development of musculature relative to bodily frame as well
as general overall bodily proportions. That being the case,
some features of men that make them powerfully built will be
irrelevant in judging that property in women—for example,
the relative breadth of shoulders to waist and hips and the con-
sequent shape of the torso. And it is precisely this sort of disparity that can, as we noticed earlier, make a PQD relative to
sorts of "objects."

Now it is impossible for the pyramids to be strong-looking
in the way that Moore's figures are, and impossible for a man's
face to be craggy-looking in the way that a mountain ridgeline
is. But it is not impossible for a woman to have slim hips and
broad shoulders, any more than it is for a man to have narrow
shoulders and a pear-shaped torso. And it is even possible for
a woman to be very powerfully built (in just the way that a
man of that size and frame would be). In such a case, however,

---

[15] Obviously, we *can* explicitly relativize a property of *quantitative*
degree to a specified sort of thing. Thus we can think of someone being
more powerful *for a woman* than someone else is *for a man*, because
there is always the possibility of determining one statistical range of
powerfulness for males and one for females. A crucial difference between
a PQD and a property of *quantitative* degree is that the relativizing of
the latter is never *necessitated* by two or more "objects" to which it
applies but which are incomparable with respect to it.

not only would the *woman* not be beautiful, but her powerfulness of build would not be beautiful. In fact, it is even doubtful
how appropriate it would be to call her "powerfully built"
without, at least, putting scare quotes around the term. At any
rate, no matter how we must describe her build, the way she
is built is not a beautiful property of her; for the way she is
built makes her rather freakish. Of course, such a woman is
certainly not *misshapen*, like a naturally deformed person or an
artificially mangled one. She is not quite *badly shaped*. And it is
not even accurate to say that she has the *wrong shape*. But it is
certainly true that there is *something wrong about* her shape, just
as—and in no greater or lesser degree— there is something
wrong about the shape of the narrow-shouldered and pear-
torsoed man. What is wrong is precisely that her torso is very
powerfully built (for a man). For just that reason the very
powerful build of her torso is not a beautiful property of her.

Much the same can be said of the property of elegance.
Naturally, both men and women can be extremely elegant, and
beautiful because of that; Van Dyke painted hardly anything
but beautifully elegant people. Now elegance is a function of
fineness—fineness in the fabrics of one's dress, in the work-
manship of one's clothing, fineness of manners, of movement,
of bearing. It is opposed to coarseness and vulgarity of all kinds.
Apart from purely physical qualities, like an elegant neck or
elegant legs, elegance in a person is due chiefly to manners,
tastes, and trappings. That being the case, we can see how
elegance can have a female and a male variety. For the manners,
preferences, and paraphernalia of women and men in all
societies I know of are clearly and definitely differentiated by sex.

What does this fact mean for our purposes? No matter how
beautifully elegant the Duchess of Winthropchester is, if the
Earl of Westumberland always dresses, moves, and behaves

just like her, that "elegance" is not a beautiful property of him. Note that "elegance" here deserves scare quotes just because it is not so clear that the Earl is "really" elegant. But, as with the man-shaped woman, it is too facile to claim simply that the Earl is not elegant. For it is surely true that the Earl is extremely elegant (in a feminine way). What prevents this "elegance" in the Earl from being a beautiful property of his is that it is precisely in virtue of this "elegance" that something is "wrong" with the Earl. Of course, what is "wrong" may be perfectly harmless, even to the Earl; and it may be tolerated and "understood" by everyone in his circle. These circumstances do not, however, mitigate the fact that the Earl is disturbed and confused at a deep emotional level.

The situation would be different, to be sure, if the Earl were a female impersonator in an established tradition of that theatrical form and were to act as he does only on clearly defined theatrical occasions. Then the elegance he gets into his performance might indeed be beautiful. Such extreme elegance in an impersonated character would not go to make the *Earl* beautifully elegant, but it might well serve to make his *performance* beautiful by reason of its high degree of intelligence and skill. But that is a topic for later discussion.

The property of regularity exhibits yet a different variety of relativity. Formal French gardens like the ones at Chateau Villandry are beautiful in part because of their high degree of regularity, the "high degree" deriving to some extent from the size and complexity of the gardens. But, while regularity is a virtue of French formal gardens, it is the opposite of a virtue in so-called English gardens, such as the one in Munich. Now regularity applies to gardens, either French or English, in virtue of the same *sorts* of properties: the placement of vegetation, the varieties of vegetation used, the style of tending the vegetation, etc. Thus it is probable that any English garden is less regular than any formal French garden. So the two kinds of gardens are clearly comparable with respect to the property of regularity. Yet it is also true that a very regular English garden is going to be considerably less regular than an irregular French garden. In other words, the scales of regularity for English gardens and formal French gardens occupy, respectively, the lower and upper ends of some sort of "absolute" scale of regularity for gardens. It is also important to note that, because regularity is a *defect* of English gardens, the more regular such a garden is, the less likely it is to be beautiful. This is not to say that such a garden will not be beautiful; it is to say that its regularity would not count in favor of its being beautiful.

19. *Beauty of Sound*

No one has ever disputed, I think, that sounds can be beautiful. In this section I want only to illustrate how it is that aural beauty substantiates NTB.

We often regard melodies, or the passages, chords, and harmonic progressions of compositions, or even whole compositions as beautiful. But single notes in isolation can be beautiful, too, in the sense of beautifully sung or played. Thus sometimes a note that is sung or played expressively is more beautiful than one that is sung or played mechanically or lifelessly. Similarly, a high note that "shatters" or "fuzzes out" on some sound equipment is more beautifully reproduced,[16] because more *clearly* reproduced, on better sound

[16] In these cases the adverbial form of "beautiful" has nothing essential to do with the adverbial form that is used to modify "beautiful

equipment. In general, clarity is a PQD making for beauty in both the performance and the electronic reproduction of music, from single notes to whole operas. Of course, this point must be taken as assuming a correct interpretation of "clarity" in individual cases. An electronic system might reproduce the sound of played music in such a way that certain sound blends, which are naturally produced in standard concert halls and which the composer was trying to achieve, are lost and the sounds of individual voices or instruments stand out too strongly. What cases of this sort show is that clarity of sound, like other PQDs we've discussed, is relative to a variety of sorts of sound and that, with respect to certain sorts of sound, clarity can be the very opposite of a beautiful property. For if the individual sounds composing an *intended* blend are played or reproduced very clearly, this clarity may be a *defect* in the performance or reproduction.

Let us turn, though, to more complex forms of beauty in interpretation, performance, and composition. Beauty of music is probably harder to describe than visual beauty, and not merely for nonmusical persons. There are few descriptions of sound that are not metaphorical. "Loud," "fast," "slow" are some, but they do not signify PQDs. In fact, I can think of no PQD of sound that is not metaphorically described in its *standard* description. Some are described by metaphorical adjectives of light such as "brilliant," "clear," "shimmering,"

---

predicates" (see above, p. 16). This adverbial form can be painlessly translated into what I am taking as the canonical form for attributions of beauty thus:

    a) "The note is sung beautifully (because very expressively)" = "The way the note is sung is beautiful (because very expressive)";

    b) "The sound is reproduced beautifully (because very clearly)" = "The way the sound is produced is beautiful (because very clear)."

"glowing," "radiant." Some by metaphors of temperature like "warm" and "cool." Others by metaphors of space like "grand," "voluminous," "lofty," "spacious." Still others by metaphors of motion: "fluid," "graceful," "sweeping," "soaring," "still." Most are described by anthropomorphic metaphors like "expressive," "gentle," "bold," "sultry," "languid," "passionate," "exalted," "dignified," "stately," "noble," "tender," "sad," "gay," "joyful," "light-hearted." Most of these properties are rather ordinary ones. Often music, more than other things, will be beautiful in ways that elude description. I have never been able to fathom, for example, why the light clashes of cymbals in the *Sanctus* of Berlioz's *Requiem* are so gorgeous. But the fact that words fail us so often in locating the beauty of music is a reflection of the poverty of our standard aural vocabulary, not a sign that there are often no beautiful PQDs with respect to which music is beautiful.

It seems pointless to give examples of music exemplifying the above described properties, since it is fairly obvious that the results would be simply the ones specified by NTB. The reader may most readily convince himself of this by listening to or recalling music beautiful because of any of those properties and then imagining or recalling performances of the same music in which precisely that property is not as strikingly or eloquently brought out. It will surely come as no shock to realize that the beauty of the music *in the relevant respect* is, in the second set of cases, diminished.

20. *Beauties of Taste, Smell, and Touch*

No one, so far as I know, has ever questioned that there are visual and aural beauties. There is no consensus of opinion, however, on whether tastes, smells, and feels (as in "the feel of silk") can be beautiful. Since many philosophers interested in beauty have been Platonists suspicious of the senses, some of them have either denied that beauty belongs in these realms or indicated that such beauty as is found there is somehow "inferior." Even twentieth-century men-on-the-street are apt to balk at the suggestion of there being gustatory, olfactory, or tactile beauty. It is, of course, a consequence of NTB that such varieties of beauty do indeed exist, for tastes, odors, and feels can be described in terms of PQDs. And it is also possible to explain, on the basis of NTB, why such beauty seems at least "marginal," if not "inferior."

A little reflection will yield to most people examples of tastes, odors, or feels that have forced from them a judgment of beauty: the sweetness of fresh-picked corn, the tanginess of a sun-ripened tomato, the smoothness of a good scotch, the pungency of pine needles, the sweetness of a rose, the smoothness of a finely sanded board, the luxuriant feel of fine velvet, the sensuous feel of deep, thick fur. Here, as elsewhere, only the very highest degrees of these qualities warrant the judgment of beauty. And yet it is clearly true for me, and I imagine for most others, that encounters with these sorts of beauty are much less frequent than with, say, visual beauty. Part of the reason stems from the nature of contemporary civilization. The range of odors that one will encounter on a farm or in the wild is naturally very much greater than in a noxious city or in a deliberately deodorized suburb. Also, it takes more money, time, and effort than most people can or want to spend to find oases in the gustatory desert that modern methods of growing, processing, and merchandising food have put us in. Most things we eat are, in fact, relatively tasteless. And, finally, the twentieth-century disappearance of handcrafts and nonmechanized farming has deprived most of the population of a large range of tactile experiences. This factor has simply been added to our general and long-standing cultural antipathy toward feeling things. We are, in short, relatively inexperienced at tasting, smelling, and feeling qualities of things. And since we can judge that a thing possesses a very high degree of a quality only if we have a significant range of experiences to use as a standard of comparison, we in this culture are by and large unqualified to judge as either beautiful or unbeautiful the way most things taste, smell, and feel.

Yet, for all that, I think there is a deeper reason why beauty of taste, touch, and smell is so rare in our experience. There is an immense number of words, in the languages I am acquainted with, for visible properties. There is even a large number of standard words for audible properties, metaphorical though most of them are. But there are very few standard terms, metaphorical or not, for qualities of taste, touch, or smell. Therefore, to be very specific in our descriptions of these qualities we are forced to name them after the things possessing the qualities: "orange-flavored," "chocolate-flavored," "winey-tasting," "a watermelony smell," "leathery smell," "velvety feel," "sandpapery feel." Yet there is evidence that such descriptions are vague in the same way that "strawberryish look" or "Southern California-ish look" are as descriptions of a new variety of berry or an unfamiliar landscape. That is, they refer to *clusters* of properties. For example, we can agree that orange blossoms, roses, and sweet peas all have, characteristically, sweet fragrances. Nevertheless, they don't all smell alike; there is a kind of "wildness" or "sharpness" that distinguishes the orange blossom from the "blander" rose and the more "astringent" sweet pea, whereas the last has "lightness" or "delicacy" that contrasts with "heaviness" or "sultriness" of the rose and the "nervousness" or "quickness" of the orange blossom. I expect hardly anyone to nod assent to the descriptions in the previous sentence, yet I imagine that most other people can also detect separate qualities in fragrances that have no standard descriptions, but for the discrimination of which terms like "rosey fragrance" are not useful. What this linguistic fact means, then, is that since NTB understands the beauty of any "object" in terms of the PQDs of that "object," the fewer PQDs that a sort of "object" has that we have "access" to, the fewer the opportunities there will be for us to perceive beauty in that sort of "object."

In making this assertion, I am not presupposing any thesis concerning the "effect" of language on perception. I am simply leaving it open whether we have trouble discriminating qualities of taste, touch, or feel "because" our languages are poor in the relevant vocabularies, whether the languages are poor "because," as a type of animal, human beings have very limited discriminatory abilities with respect to such qualities, or whether human beings, having had, at one time at least, perfectly adequate abilities to discriminate as many qualities of taste, touch, or feel as exist, never found it necessary (evolutionarily speaking) to encode these discriminations in language. It might even be that there simply *exist* fewer PQDs of tastes, smells, and feels than there are of visible objects or music, though I am far from clear what it would take to verify such a hypothesis. One thing is clear, though: we generally discriminate fewer properties of taste, touch, or smell than we do visible and audible properties, and we therefore have fewer opportunities to encounter beauties of those senses.

However unsubtle our terms for qualities of taste, touch, and smell may be, we can nevertheless treat them as signifying genuine properties, even if complex properties. These properties divide themselves into two categories: (1) properties like *saltiness, sweetness, acridity, pungency, luxuriance, fuzziness, softness,* etc., and (2) properties like *being orange-blossomy, being chocolaty, being burnt-wood-like, being winesapy,* etc. It should be obvious that the properties in category (1) are severely limited in number, but that there are as many properties in category (2) as there are kinds of things that have a taste, a smell, or a feel. It is also obvious, I take it, that properties in both categories can be possessed in nonenumerable degrees; that is, they are all PQDs. I will try to show now how properties of each category exemplify NTB.

The principle of relativity of PQDs is nowhere better illustrated than in the realm of taste, touch, and smell. Sweetness, for example, is relative to such diverse things as oranges, corn, strawberries, milk, cucumbers. On the other hand, there seems to be a scale of sweetness that ranks even relative sweetness according to itself. On this scale pure sugar and honey would have the highest degrees of sweetness. One has no trouble admitting that the highest degrees of sweetness, both relative and "absolute," do make for beauty of taste. Properties like saltiness, sourness, acridity, however, immediately raise some problems, chiefly because these properties are frequently disliked by some people. Naturally, certain instances of these properties, as in sour milk, salty soup, and acrid pipe tobacco, pose no problems for NTB, because they are *defects* of what they qualify. But the salty taste of some pickles, for example, is not a defect; they are supposed to be that way. Yet some people don't like them, and just because they are too salty for them. According to NTB, however, the saltiness of the pickles ought to be one of their beautiful properties. Similarly, acridity in the smell of burning fall leaves is not a defect, deficiency, or lack. And while some people like such a smell the more pungently acrid it is, other people cannot bear it—or indeed any acridity of smell. But how can people dislike what, according to NTB, must be beautiful? Likewise, sourness is not a defect of a lemon's taste; on the contrary, less sour lemons are often dry and bland, qualities that are defects of lemons, making sourness one of their virtues. Yet some persons never like the sourness of lemons, and others like it only occasionally. And we can even see now, looking back at sweetness, that the sweetest things there are, and therefore the most beautiful things with respect to sweetness, are often distasteful to some people. Despite these facts, it seems an unassailable axiom that the beautiful is, preeminently, that which is enjoyable. Similar problems arise in connection with qualities of touch like sliminess. Sliminess is almost universally disliked, and yet there are things, like garden slugs, that are slimy but are by no means defective or deficient because of it. Indeed, being slimy is a sign of health in slugs. The problem for NTB is to explain how what must, on its account, be beautiful can nevertheless be distasteful or repulsive.

The same problem comes up with regard to the second category of properties. It seems unassailable that the more almond-tasting an almond is, the better it is, and that the most almond-tasting ones—the ones "packed with flavor" or "bursting with flavor"—are beautifully so. The same goes for a winesapy taste, an artichoke-taste, a piney smell, a lemony smell. There are also properties of this category that are the "appearance" of defects or of deficiencies, either relative or absolute: green-banana taste, sour-apple taste, rotten-potato smell. But there are some properties that are neither defects or deficiencies nor their "appearance" but are nevertheless universally disliked, such as a lemon-rind taste, a peach-seed taste, a urine smell, the characteristic "sluggy" feel. As with properties in category

(1), anything possessing these properties would seem to be *less*, not more, beautiful the greater the degree to which they are present in the thing.

21. *Qualifications for Judging Beauty*

My first reaction to the apparent threat to NTB posed by these properties of taste, touch, and smell is to doubt that most people, including myself, are qualified to judge whether these sorts of properties provide counterexamples to NTB. And that is because most persons' experiences with tastes, odors, and feels of these sorts are extremely limited, for obvious reasons. I, for one, have *never* felt a slug, and I've tasted a peach seed only once. As I indicated earlier, however, fairly extensive experience of a property is absolutely required before the comparative degrees of it can be judged. We can imagine a person who, like an infant, was used only to bland foods and who did not like the taste of oranges the first few times he tried them. But no one would think that such a person, after two or three tastes of oranges, would be qualified to judge excellence of flavor in orange juice. Indeed, even if he *liked* the taste immediately, his experience at first would not enable him to discriminate degrees of orange-tastingness.

I am suggesting that the way to understand our not liking certain properties of taste, touch, or smell is on the model of the infant-like person innocent of the taste of oranges: we simply are not qualified to judge beauty or nonbeauty with respect to those properties. Of course, in some respects some of the disagreeable properties mentioned are not like the taste of oranges. For with respect to the latter there exist many persons who do not dislike oranges and who are able to say that

66

the very highest degree of the characteristic orange taste is a beautiful taste. But with respect to urine and skunk smells, the feel of slugs and the taste of peach seeds, there seems to be no one who *is* qualified to perceive a comparative qualitative ranking within each property. Still, we cannot claim *a priori* that such a ranking is impossible. For we can easily imagine how for certain specialized purposes in science or industry some people might develop a fine discrimination of qualitative differences with respect to urine smells, the slimy feel of slugs, or the taste of lemon rinds.

As for disliking high degrees of saltiness, of sourness, or of sweetness, it is easier to see how by reason of such dislike a person is disqualified from judging them either beautiful or not. Here we can take clearer examples from other sensory properties. It is not difficult to imagine a person whose eyes literally hurt when he looks at bright colors and who therefore must always take care to surround himself with pastels. Such a person would presumably be able to judge beauty with respect to any color in the less (absolutely) vivid range, but not with respect to the (relative) vividness of even the spectral colors. In this case the pain of seeing vivid spectral colors functions as an obstacle in perceiving their beauty. And a similar situation obtains, but much more frequently, with respect to properties of taste, touch, and smell.

A natural objection to this line of argument is that since what is beautiful is always enjoyable (likeable, pleasant, agreeable), these various dislikes are actually counterexamples to NTB. And, of course, if this objection has any force, then the whole structure of NTB is completely shattered. For the dislike of properties of taste, touch, and smell is by no means the only kind of dislike available. Some persons dislike green, or blue, or red; dislike pale colors, dark colors, bright colors; dislike mountains, plains, hills, lakes, seashores—the list is endless. But if the fact that some person finds a whole category of "object" or some property or other disagreeable is allowed to tell against that sort of "object" or those properties being beautiful, then there will surely remain no PQD of a thing at all that, even if present in an extreme degree, is beautiful.

What is at issue here is the precise nature of the relation between the beauty of anything and the enjoyment (delight, pleasure, agreeableness, etc.) customarily associated with beauty. Now I think everyone must admit that it is not only no contradiction, but that it might often be the case, that a thing is beautiful with respect to some PQD and that some person finds that thing, precisely in that respect, disagreeable or in some way unpleasant. Furthermore, that person may find the thing disagreeable in that respect because he finds every instance of that PQD, or every instance with a relatively high degree of that PQD, at least as relativized to a sort of "object," similarly unpleasant. For if there were no such possibilities, there would be no point in saying that so-and-so is insensitive to the beauties of, say, Berlioz, of Renaissance chamber music, of succulents, of desert landscapes, of collie dogs, or of Abstract Expressionist painting. And yet we are often forced to recognize such insensitivities. Of course, a person may have such an insensitivity and remain quite neutral toward its "objects," for the insensitivity may be due solely to the lack of experience and knowledge of that kind of "object." But the insensitivity may also accompany, and even be the result of, an active dislike of "objects" of that kind. And thus it is not true that *everyone must* find a beautiful thing agreeable, or even find agreeable the respects in which a beautiful thing is beautiful.

It is therefore possible that X be beautiful with respect to F

and that some person find X disagreeable precisely with respect to F. But then it is possible that X be beautiful with respect to F and that I find X disagreeable precisely with respect to F. And yet there is *something wrong* in *my* saying that blue color on the chair is beautiful but I dislike it. What exactly is wrong, however, cannot be that I am contradicting myself or implying a contradiction; "X is beautiful" does not entail "X is agreeable to me." In the same way "It is raining" does not entail "I believe it is raining"; but there is *something wrong* with saying that it is raining but I don't believe it. What is wrong in the latter case is that my saying and meaning that it is raining implies (no matter what "implies" here *really* means) that I believe it is raining. And likewise my saying and meaning (that is, "judging") that X is beautiful implies that I find X agreeable at least in the respect that X is beautiful. It is, in other words, a necessary condition of a person's *judging* something as beautiful with respect to F that he find it agreeable with respect to F.

We can rephrase the preceding point in this way: a person can judge an "object" X as beautiful with respect to its property F only if he finds X agreeable with respect to F. From this it follows that if a person does not find X agreeable with respect to F, he cannot judge X beautiful with respect to F. *A fortiori*, a person who finds all instances of F or a certain subset of these instances—say, all those in which F is present to a noticeable degree—disagreeable cannot judge any of those instances beautiful. But, of course, finding all or a large subset of the instances of F to be disagreeable does not *necessitate* judging F to be, in any of these instances, not beautiful. In other words, if I find something about an "object" disagreeable, I cannot judge it to be beautiful, but neither am I obliged to judge it to be not beautiful. Furthermore, I think that if a person finds an instance of a property disagreeable *because he either finds all instances of that property disagreeable or finds a subset of those instances disagreeable*, then he cannot be taken to have grounds for judging it to be not beautiful, because he is not qualified to make judgments of beauty (or nonbeauty) with respect to the instances, or the subset of them, of that property.

The argument for the last claim is this. If a person is qualified to make judgments of beauty with respect to property F, then he is able to discriminate between beautiful and nonbeautiful instances of F. And if he can, then *generally*, if he perceives a beautiful instance of F, he will judge it to be beautiful, and if he perceives a nonbeautiful instance of F, he will judge it to be nonbeautiful. But if it is known that a person will find all instances of F, or those instances in which F is present in a noticeable degree, to be disagreeable, then it is known that he will not be able to judge any instances of F to be beautiful, whether they are so or not. And if he cannot, then it is not the case that *generally*, if he perceives a beautiful instance of F, he will judge it to be beautiful. If that is so, moreover, then he is not able to discriminate between beautiful and nonbeautiful instances of F, and he is therefore not qualified to judge beauty or nonbeauty with respect to F. But if he is not qualified, then he cannot be taken to have grounds for judging an instance of F as not beautiful.

The implications of this conclusion are far-reaching. One consequence is that if we dislike the characteristic taste of lemon rinds, the characteristic odor of skunks on the defensive (offensive?), or the characteristic feel of garden slugs, we are not entitled to use these properties either to confirm or to disconfirm NTB. A person who does not like very salty-, very sweet-, or very sour-tasting things cannot use these properties as counterexamples to NTB. Likewise, people who because of their family or educational background find, say, bright pure colors generally offensive cannot use the vividness of such colors as counterexamples to NBT. But by the same token neither can persons able to enjoy the beauty of color only in pure bright colors use subtly toned colors against the theory. People who do not in general like any degree of willowy elegance in female bodies and who therefore prefer females with a low degree of such elegance cannot use as disconfirming evidence of NTB the property of willowy elegance. And, of course, those who dislike Rubens-like sensuousness and voluptousness in females and judge such females to be in no respect beautiful cannot be considered qualified to judge beauty with respect to these properties, and their judgments cannot provide counterexamples to NTB.

22. *Intellectual Beauty*

There is a variety of beauty that is frequently mentioned in discussions of the subject, unfortunately with respect only to a single sort of example: elegant mathematical proofs. An elegant proof is one that is simple, clear, direct, neat, and a beautiful proof is one that excells with respect to any or all of these properties. But a beautiful proof is only one example of a whole category that I will call "intellectual beauty."

Generally speaking, it is the *products* of the intellect, exhibiting certain properties, that are thought to be beautiful with respect to those properties. Thus a theory may be beautiful if it is extraordinarily simple or powerful. The exposition of a difficult theory can also be beautiful if it is especially clear or insightful. A musical composition may be beautiful if it is extremely inventive. An interpretation—that is, performance—

of a musical composition may be beautiful if it is especially penetrating, sensitive, or spirited. A performance on stage can be beautiful for its exceptional insight into the portrayed character.

Another notable variety of intellectual beauty is beauty with respect to skillfulness. Thus, whenever something is done with extraordinary skill, it can be said to be done beautifully: jumping a horse, making a high dive, pruning a tree, escorting a project through a bureaucratic maze. It is important in such instances to distinguish the beauty due to the skillful way a thing is done from the beauty of the result. Some things done beautifully are also, and necessarily, beautiful in other ways. Skillful dives or jumps are also beautiful because of their grace or their smoothness of movement. A skillfully done arabesque will generally *look* beautiful, too, although this is not always so. (Consider it done by a person with a bad line—too short a torso and poor extension.) Sometimes, however, what is beautifully done does not issue in anything beautiful in other respects. A beautiful portrayal of Iago does not produce beauty in Iago. A beautiful performance of Cinderella's stepsisters in Ashton's ballet *cannot* produce beautifully graceful or elegant movements on the stage. This point may provide one solution to the "problem of the ugly" in art, the question how art that is "of the ugly" can have any aesthetic value, when "aesthetic value" means "beauty." The grotesque, deformed, and obscene obviously can be depicted or portrayed with remarkable skill, imaginativeness, or vividness and hence beautifully without thereby making the grotesque, the deformed, or the obscene themselves beautiful.

Of course, people who play, draw, perform, dive, or otherwise act beautifully, or who conceive beautiful theories and beautiful proofs, who write beautifully clear expositions, are

72

themselves skillful, inventive, imaginative and possess acute, powerful, precise, clear minds. Are *people* also called beautiful because of these "intellectual" properties? Yes. For we know, or can conceive of, beautiful swimmers, divers, jumpers, actors, draughtsmen, of persons with beautifully clear, acute, or inventive minds. It is by virtue of their beautiful "intellectual" properties that people can do things beautifully.

23. *Beauty and Utility*

The last point brings to mind a category of phenomena that must, according to NTB, be examples of beauty, but that are not even recognized in some traditional theories as bona fide cases of beauty. They are, however, regarded as the central (and sometimes only) instances of beauty by traditional theorists who, like Socrates, have conceived of beauty as "utility" (occasionally termed "suitability," "appropriateness," "aptness," "fittingness," or "function").[17] We sometimes talk of a thing or a material "doing beautifully," meaning that it will serve very well for a certain purpose. For example, certain kinds of coals may cook beautifully, knives may cut beautifully, cloth may polish beautifully, or a certain soil may serve beautifully for growing tobacco, certain trees for making masts, reeds for weaving baskets. Frequently, though not necessarily, something beautiful may be the result of a thing's serving a purpose beautifully. If certain soil serves beautifully for growing tobacco, the tobacco is perhaps *likely* to be beautiful. But baskets made of reeds that serve beautifully for basket

[17] See Tatarkiewicz, I, 98 and 102ff., for the origins of this notion and Socrates's relation to it. Tatarkiewicz's work, both volumes, is very helpful in tracing the vicissitudes of this idea down to modern times.

weaving might just as easily be unbeautiful as beautiful. Thus a thing or material that serves beautifully does not do so because the *product* of the "service" is beautiful. When something or material serves beautifully for the purpose of ϕ-ing, however, it follows that that thing or material is beautiful for ϕ-ing.

I have already said how NTB comprehends "objects" (other than PQDs) that are beautiful. Now I have to try to show how NTB also comprehends "objects" that are *beautiful for ϕ-ing*. The latter appear, superficially, to elude the grasp of NTB. But, as we did for other "objects," we can ask of "objects" beautiful *for* something: "With respect to what is X beautiful for ϕ-ing?" and "What about X makes it beautiful for ϕ-ing?"[18] Just as with other beautiful "objects," these questions do not always immediately yield answers in terms of PQDs or even in terms of properties. For example, if one asks about one of those cheese slicers that look like toy hacksaws "What about the slicer makes it beautiful for slicing cheese?" one can get as an answer "Its thin blade." But then we can ask what about the thin blade makes it beautiful for cheese slicing and get the answer "The great ease ('easiness') with which it cuts through the cheese." In like manner we can discover that coals are beautiful for cooking because of the evenness and thoroughness of the way they are heated. A knife that cuts jungle underbrush beautifully does so because it is beautifully (extremely) sharp. Beautiful soil may be extremely rich. Beautiful timbers

---

[18] Notice that this question is not *exactly* like the earlier question "What is beautiful about X?" which seems in the instant cases grammatically infelicitous. Note, however, that the "makes it beautiful" form can be appropriately put either to "objects" that are beautiful *for something* or to "objects" that are beautiful, but not beautiful *for* anything.

for making masts may be so because of their great straightness and solidity. Beautiful reeds for basket weaving may be extremely pliable and yet extremely tough.

The question arises, of course, whether everything that serves beautifully for some purpose always does so, ultimately or proximately, with respect to the sort of PQDs specified by NTB. For the kinds of examples given above, the answer seems to be yes—that is, for examples of serving a purpose that belong to *kinds* of things, whether artificial or natural, that standardly or normally serve a certain *kind* of purpose. But there are also examples of things serving purposes that are *not* normal or standard purposes for things of that sort. What about them? What about, for instance, the particular book that, I found after trying many others, does beautifully for evening up the legs on my typing table? In this case there would seem to be no property of the book that, being possessed in a high degree, makes it serve its purpose beautifully. Rather, it seems that one of its properties of *quantitative* degree, namely its size, is what makes it beautiful. And, furthermore, it is not its being of great size, but its being *just the right size*, neither too big nor too small, that makes it "do" beautifully. Or what about the stick with the chewed gum on the end that serves beautifully for retrieving the dollar under the grate?

The above sorts of examples are not counterexamples to NTB. For what is true of both the book under the table leg and the stick with the chewing gum is that both are, to a high degree, *suitable* to the purpose they serve and, indeed, more suitable than other objects and devices that would also serve, but less than beautifully, the same purposes. It is, in other words, the PQD of *suitability*, or what is in old-fashioned language sometimes called *fittingness*, that grounds the beautiful functioning of the book and the stick. We can even turn this point back on our earlier examples of serving beautifully and see that all of them serve beautifully with respect to their high degree of suitability for their purposes. Indeed, it seems to me analytically true that any "object" that serves a purpose beautifully does so because of its very high suitability for that purpose. But analytic truth is truth; and hence the whole class of "objects" beautifully serving a purpose corroborates NTB. In other words, the beauty in "objects" *beautiful for* something can be reduced to beautiful PQDs just as can the beauty of other "objects."

The important thing about the last point is that a kind of beauty, which on the surface seems so different from common-place sorts of natural and artistic beauty, can be comprehended by a theory that also comprehends both of the latter sorts of beauty as well as "intellectual" beauty. For this fact (1) justifies to some degree the long tradition of "functionalism" in the theory of beauty by showing it to be based on sound intuitions and (2) refutes the common allegation that "functional" beauty of the sort discussed in this section is called "beautiful" in a merely metaphorical or extended sense. Indeed, I take it as self-evident that the success of NTB—or of any compre-hensive theory of beauty—would be enough to discredit the old and popular notion that the reason "beautiful" applies to so many diverse varieties of "objects" is that it is radically ambiguous.

24. *Beauty and Goodness*

In the discussion thus far I have suggested several times that beauty and goodness are closely related. Traditionally theorists of beauty have noted a close relationship between the two ideas. Some philosophers have even identified the two notions. Others have claimed that they are coextensive, that whatever is beautiful is good and the converse.[19] Neither of these theses is correct; the truth is more complex and various than either of these theses make it out to be. For some classes of beautiful "objects" (and of good "objects") there is no connection between beauty and goodness. For the others, though the connection is close, it is different for different kinds of beautiful "objects."

If I say the hills are beautiful because of their vivid green or vivid golden color, if I say the bull against the sky or the bare hills in the afternoon sun on a clear day are very solid-looking, I imply nothing about whether the hills are good hills or the bulls good bulls. The only connection between these sorts of beauties and goodness is that what is beautiful is presumably good to look at.

But a bull may be beautiful because it is so very strong-looking and healthy-looking. And then it follows that the bull is also *good-looking*, and good-looking with respect to some properties that make it beautiful. Note, though, that if a bull is good-looking with respect to PQDs F and G, it may or may not be the case that it is beautiful with respect to F or G. "Good-looking" and "beautiful," even when applied by virtue of the same properties, mark different segments of the degree scales of those properties. It is not always clear how these different segments are related, however. Sometimes "good-looking" marks a segment just below the "beautiful" segment

---

[19] The scholastic philosophers William of Auvergne and William of Auxerre, according to Tatarkiewicz, identified "good" and "beautiful" (II, 219), while Aquinas, among others, thought the concepts were merely coextensive (II, 246). Again, Tatarkiewicz's two volumes (*passim*) are very informative on this whole topic.

of the scale, and sometimes it marks a segment that begins somewhat lower than the "beautiful" segment but includes the "beautiful" segment. The difference is analogous to the difference, on the scale *poor/below-average/average/above-average/excellent*, between "above-average" on the one hand and "above-average *or* excellent" on the other. In the latter case, of course, it follows from the fact that a bull is beautiful with respect to being strong-looking and being healthy-looking that it is good-looking; in the former case it does not follow. Which of these meanings "good-looking" has in a particular case either is not clear at all or is supplied by contextual cues.

The same point applies to all cases of good-lookingness, whether in people, dogs, pine trees, or automobiles. And what holds for the relation between "beautiful" and "good-looking" applies analogously to the relation between "beautiful" and "good-tasting," "good-smelling," and "having a good feel," as said, for example, of a firm apple or a smooth fabric.

The way that "good-looking" works vis-à-vis "beautiful" provides the key for a large set of instances of goodness and beauty. Note that "good" applied to, say, a strawberry holds of it in precisely those respects that "beautiful" would hold of it, namely, with respect to its juiciness, ripeness, vividness of color (relative to its special redness), sweetness, and flavorfulness (having the particular strawberryish flavor). Similarly, a good theory is one that is at least *reasonably* simple and *reasonably* powerful. A good performance is one that is at least *reasonably* skillful and insightful. Even with things being *good for* some purpose or other, "goodness for" applies with respect to just those properties that "beautiful for" might. In general, wherever "goodness" applies with respect to PQDs, it marks either a range of degrees just below the range marked by "beautiful" or that range plus the range marked by "beautiful."

But, in any case, the beauty of any "object" that exists with respect to any of the good-making PQDs of that "object" consists in, at least, *excellence* with respect to that property and, at most, *surpassing excellence* with respect to that property, where "excellence" means "more than mere goodness."

I have already noted that beauty in some properties, especially visual but also aural properties, has nothing essential to do with the goodness of the "objects" that they qualify. They are connected to goodness only by being good to look at or good to hear. On the other hand, the goodness that an object has if it is a good one of that *sort* of thing exists ultimately in virtue of PQDs of that "object," as does the goodness that an "object" has if it is good for some purpose or other. It is worth noticing that there is a variety of goodness that has nothing essential to do with beauty. That is the goodness that is roughly the same as *being beneficial to* or *for*. It is in this sense that rain and sunshine are good (for the crops, for human beings), that the flooding of the Nile was good for the ancient Egyptians, that exercise is good for house pets, that shade is good for ferns. In no case of this sort is the "object" that is good, or the properties in virtue of which it is good, necessarily related to beauty.

It is instructive to note how my conclusions about the relation between beauty and goodness compare with those of the most influential modern philosopher of beauty, Immanuel Kant. Unlike most ancient and medieval philosophers, Kant made a radical distinction between a judgment of beauty and a judgment of goodness. The distinction ultimately boils down to the doctrine that the latter judgments are "objective" and "cognitive," and therefore express *knowledge about objects*, whereas the former are "subjective" and merely "aesthetical," and therefore express *feelings of subjects*. What is interesting, though, is that Kant recognized the fact that beauty is attributed to things both in virtue of their *utility* (what they are *good for*) and in virtue of their possessing qualities according to which they are *good specimens* of their respective kinds. Moreover, Kant admitted that the judgments of these varieties of goodness—that is, being good for something and being a good specimen of a kind—are indeed objective because they are determined by concepts, namely, the concept of the "external" *purpose* that a thing is good for and the concept of the *kind* of thing to which it belongs. To square these facts with his subjective theory of beauty Kant distinguishes between two "kinds" of beauty: "free" or "self-subsistent" beauty, on the one hand, and "dependent," "conditioned," or "adherent" beauty, on the other. It seems clear to me that under "free beauty" Kant would include just those beauties that I said above are unrelated to goodness except in being good to look at or listen to (a sort of goodness that Kant, too, I'm sure, would concede to them).[20]

It is obvious from the Kantian text that in the part of the *Critique of Judgment* dealing with beauty Kant is interested chiefly in free beauty. And it is his doctrines about free beauty that have been most influential in modern aesthetics. In fact, beauty in modern times has come to be commonly identified with "free" beauty, and philosophers have dropped all interest in "adherent beauty." What NTB does against Kantian doctrines is to show that there is no distinction, as Kant has drawn it, between "free" and "adherent" beauty, because *all* varieties of beauty are "determined by concepts"—indeed, by the same concept. By showing the unity among what Kant

---

[20] Immanuel Kant, *Critique of Judgment*, tr. J. H. Bernard (New York: Hafner, 1951) pp. 62–68.

had sharply separated, moreover, NTB yanks the rug out from under the chief support for the nearly universal modern faith in the splendid isolation and precious purity of everything "genuinely" aesthetic.

25. *The Problem of Moral Beauty*

Given the connections with goodness that beauty has, it is easy to see why and how some people—including some philosophers—have talked of moral beauty, that is to say, have attributed beauty to the moral virtues. And, of course, it is a consequence of NTB that virtues like kindness, honesty, faithfulness, loyalty, and reliability are beautiful properties, because they are all PQDs. At this point, however, a methodological question obtrudes itself: by what right can we even speak of *morally* beautiful persons, persons, that is, who are beautiful with respect to their moral virtues? For if we can and do unproblematically apply "beautiful" to the moral virtues, and mean thereby just what NTB says we must mean by "beautiful," then the phenomenon of moral beauty is simply further corroboration of NTB. But if "beautiful" is not properly applied to persons in this way and yet, according to NTB, it ought to be, the moral virtues would appear to constitute a set of counterexamples to NTB.

Are people, then, properly described as beautiful with respect to their virtues? Well, if we consider simply contemporary uses of the term "beautiful," the answer, I think, is no. I have never used the term to describe the moral character of a person I've known or known about. And I cannot recall hearing or seeing the term so used by my contemporaries. I presume my experience in this regard matches that of most other persons.[21] In this respect the moral virtues are quite unlike the other varieties of PQDs discussed so far as varieties of beauty. Yet what does this fact tell? For I can *imagine* using the term to apply to a person's moral character; and, when invited, so can other people I know. But how far does imagination get us? For I can also imagine, when I set my mind to it, using the terms "hot" and "cold" to describe moral character. Indeed, the linguistic imagination seems infinitely rich. There will always be those more pedestrian minds who will be unable, or who will flatly refuse, to conceive a new use of a term, as there will always be those fanciful minds who will avidly seek to stretch a word to cover new cases. The methodological problem is: Is there any way to choose either to use "beautiful" to apply to moral properties or to refuse to do so, without choosing simply to be pedestrian or to be fanciful?

I think there would not be a way were it not for an arresting fact. The fact is that a whole stream of philosophers, including Plato, Aristotle, Cicero, Plotinus, Augustine, Aquinas, Ficino, Shaftesbury, and Kant, attribute beauty to moral virtues, to "souls" or persons, apparently without embarrassment, that is, without a sense that they are doing something "linguistically odd." On the other hand, it is rare, if not impossible, to find "beautiful" used by more recent philosophers, and indeed by

[21] Sanford Thatcher has tactfully suggested to me that, in saying this, I locate myself on the depressing side of the generation gap. He believes that more or less current "hip" talk uses "beautiful" in a moral way. As my conclusions eventually will show, I am more than willing to believe that he is right, even if my own linguistic experience gives me no reason so to believe. For if Thatcher is right, NTB would appear to be more closely attuned to the *Zeitgeist* (the incoming one, not the outgoing one) than I had dared hope. The best that I can say is that any reader who does not see the existence of moral beauty as problematic may skip this section and go on to the next. My stodgier readers, with whom I (*alas!*) must identify myself, may still profit from this discussion.

any philosophers I know of in the empiricist tradition, to refer to moral character. Someone might object that, since all of the philosophers who so naturally speak of moral beauty were in some way influenced by Plato, and since Plato had a particular *theory* both of beauty and of virtue, these philosophers were committed *by their theory* to speaking of moral beauty. Thus if we reject their theory, we can reject talk of moral beauty.

One trouble with this objection is that not all of the philosophers who attribute beauty to the virtues in fact held the same theory either of beauty or of virtue. A second problem is that it is unreasonable to suppose that these philosophers simply *arbitrarily* used "beautiful" to describe virtues. In none of their writings is there a sense that "beautiful" as applied to character is in any way out of the ordinary, that they must *justify* such a use. Indeed, I. M. Crombie reports that the ancient Greek word for "beautiful" (*kalos*) was the *standard* word for the highest moral virtue.[22] Evidently, then, the linguistic propriety of applying "beautiful" to moral virtues has changed over time: before the nineteenth century such application was common in a philosophical tradition ultimately supported by a completely standard and ordinary usage, but since then this usage has been quite extraordinary in both vulgar and philosophical language.

---

[22] *An Examination of Plato's Doctrines* (London: Routledge and Kegan Paul, 1962), I, 205. Crombie also suggests, in accordance with contemporary prejudice, that this constitutes a separate *sense* of *kalos*, and that in its moral use *kalos* means just what we mean by "moral" or "morally good." As I will argue, there are reasons for doubting this opinion. That the application of "beautiful" to moral virtues was standard in ancient Greece is supported by Wladyslaw Tatarkiewicz in his *History of Aesthetics*, I, 114. Tatarkiewicz also thinks that when the Greeks applied the word we translate as "beautiful," they were using it in a different *sense* from the sense contemporaries give to their words for "beautiful" (I, 25).

There are several plausible ways of accounting for these facts. (1) The cultures that applied terms translatable as "beautiful" to moral virtues used them ambiguously to mean either "beautiful" or "moral," and although this use lived on atavistically in the language of philosophers for centuries, the ambiguity has now been extirpated. (2) The earlier use of "beautiful" was not ambiguous, but (2a) modern Western European civilization simply stopped using the terms to apply to all categories of beautiful things. In particular, (2b) it now uses words for "moral" or "morally good" to mean what words translated as "beautiful" used to mean. (3) Even though the earlier usage was not ambiguous, modern European civilization stopped applying "beautiful" to virtues because the *concept* of moral beauty fell into disuse, possibly because moral beauty became, as a type of phenomenon, very rare or nonexistent, or because it became so culturally and socially unimportant that there was no longer any need or point to talk or think about it.

What I will argue in the next section is that there are imaginable characteristics of human beings that (1) represent extremely high degrees of accepted moral virtues, but that (2) represent much more than is required of a person deemed "moral" or "good" and that (3), given what I have already said about beauty, entitle persons possessing such characteristics to be called "beautiful" with respect to them. This argument wil show hypothesis (2b) above to be false, will give considerable but by no means conclusive reason to believe that hypothesis (1) is false, and will bear out the truth of (3). The upshot will be that "beautiful" is properly applicable to moral character and, as such, both substantiates NTB and further strengthens it by (a) justifying a powerful tradition in aesthetics and ethics and (b) rediscovering a "lost" concept.

84

26. *A Defense of Moral Beauty*

When we think of a person we want to characterize as "moral," we think of a specific spectrum of virtues he possesses: honesty, responsibility, trustworthiness, respect for law, respect for the persons and property of others. When we think of a person more accurately characterizable as "good" rather than moral, we think of a different spectrum of virtues: kindness, generosity, helpfulness, compassion, and concern for others. Of course, if a person is truly "good," he will also have virtues of the "moral" person, and vice versa. Being characterizable as good rather than as moral, or as moral rather than as good, is a matter of which spectrum of virtues predominate in a person's makeup. But each need not predominate at the expense of the other. Since we don't live in a perfect universe, there must be situations in which (1) one must act either according to a "virtue of morality" or according to a "virtue of goodness," (2) one cannot do both, and (3) neither of the courses of action is clearly more *virtuous* (to use a term neutral with respect to "moral" and "good") than the other. In such situations it is the "moral" person who will choose the course of action that shows respect for the law, honesty, integrity, or responsibility; the "good" person will choose the action that is kind, generous, benevolent, or compassionate.

That there is this distinction is interesting; why there is I have no idea. The distinction is useful here chiefly because it allows us to choose two characteristic virtues—honesty and generosity—in order to analyze moral beauty. Beauty, according to NTB, is an extreme degree of a property. So a person beautiful with respect to honesty or generosity is a person who is extremely honest or extremely generous. Let us try to sketch out the popular conceptions of extreme honesty and extreme generosity.

An honest person is one who is truthful, who gives to others what is due to them and takes from others no more than is due to him. A *very* honest person is one who so conducts himself on *all* occasions, without fail. An *extremely* honest person can do more, it seems, only by being very exact in his truthfulness and exacting in the giving and taking of what is due. Now if we take such a description seriously, it begins to look as if an extremely honest person will be truthful not only beyond what most people would expect but even beyond what many people might think desirable. At the very best an extremely honest person might be pedantic and nit-picking, and at the worst he might be cruel and harmful. Likewise, the person who is extremely exacting concerning what is due to others, always returning exactly one cup of sugar exactly when promised, tends to be a person who insists on making even the simplest human contact into a series of contractual relations and is, in the end, more to be condemned for being offensive than praised for being reliable. One who at great expense and trouble to himself and others will make elaborate attempts to execute or rectify a relatively inconsequential contractual transaction (Honest Abe walking miles to return the penny change!) is at best a minor annoyance and at worst a menace to humane intercourse. Such a person is, we say, *too* honest. He is compulsively or neurotically so. There is an ungainliness and gracelessness to his virtue that is anything but beautiful.

Such is the vulgar conception of extreme honesty. Yet "too honest" is oxymoronic. How can anyone be (literally) *too* honest? Honesty is a virtue, and one of the highest. How can (true) virtue be overdone, exaggerated into something that discourages the very praise due it? How (logically) can extreme virtue depend upon traits such as rigidity, pedantry, petty cruelty, inhumanity? There is something conceptually incoherent in this notion. Such a consequence is a sign that we have not identified extreme honesty at all.

What is the ordinary notion of generosity? The generous person gives his time, energy, money, and goods to persons who are in need. The *very* generous person gives a great deal to a great many much of the time. The *extreme* degree of generosity appears to be total self-depletion, which is the logical limit of such giving. The result of extreme generosity, on this interpretation, can be destitution, death, psychic annihilation, or even moral debasement. Total self-sacrifice (à la Dostoevsky's heroine Sonya) appears to be the ultimate degree of generosity. Yet the consequences of such extreme generosity can obviously be morally disgusting. Must one lose one's life or prostitute oneself utterly for a (relatively) worthless person or to fill a (relatively) trivial need? Is there no balancing these things out? Of course there is, for all but the hopelessly foolish, benighted, or masochistic. There cannot logically be any such thing as "too much generosity," any more than there can be "too much honesty." These phrases imply that there is a degree of honesty or generosity with which there is "something wrong." But there cannot, logically speaking, be anything "wrong" with being greatly virtuous. Thus there cannot be anything about the essentially praiseworthy that refuses praise. Either honesty and generosity are not virtues, or what I have described are not the extremes of honesty and generosity. The former is false, so the latter must be true. But if so, what are the extreme degrees of honesty and generosity? I will begin answering this question by first talking about some characteristic defects in (at least moderately) honest and generous people.

One can be quite honest in a grim-faced and dour way. And to do so is not necessarily to be honest merely because otherwise one's reputation will suffer or one will be punished. One may be honest "on principle" in a dour, grim-faced way. One may tell the truth or pay a debt while fully and resentfully aware that most other people are getting away with being dishonest in similar circumstances. One may honor a free and legal contract with the bitter feeling that the partner in the contract could well have released you from obligation with negligible loss to himself and great advantage to yourself. One may act honestly with the stern realization that one has conquered one's deep and instinctive inclination to renege on an agreement or to disguise the truth. It is under such circumstances that an honest man is likely, as a bulwark against the power of his own feelings, to repeat to himself and to others that he is an honest man, a man of principle.

Such a person, supposing that he is honest in all appropriate circumstances, supposing that he is not "too honest," and also supposing that he has a like measure of the other "moral" virtues, cannot lack morality. Such a person may be as "moral" as it is possible to be. What, then, does he lack? He certainly lacks charm, grace, and joy in his "style" of being honest. And he lacks the latter virtues because his honesty does not flow naturally from him as light from a source, but must be pressed and forced out at great emotional cost. But the modern world, at least since Kant, does not see the lack of *such* virtues as a lack of *morality*. In fact, it has seemed to some to be the very condition of the moral worth of one's honesty that one *not* be honest with charm, grace, or joy. To be moral one must be honest, it often seems, against one's whole miserable nature.

There is a way of being a generous person, too, that is equally grim-faced and dour, but for different reasons. We all recognize the stereotype of the generous person who gives, not to gain a reputation or to be loved, but because she is a "good" person, who nevertheless hides her generosity behind a face of steel. She may even act anonymously in order not to reveal her generosity. She may be a tireless volunteer for charitable causes that she herself conceives, and yet she characteristically appears unsunny, unbending, and inaccessible. This is the person of whom it is said, after her death, that though she was a truly good person, she was not well liked and people frequently found it easy to forget how good she was.

Here again we have a person whose "style" lacks charm, grace, or joy. Yet the lack is not due this time to an emotional struggle to be good, for the goodness comes naturally. The lack comes from a deliberate effort to prevent the "natural" goodness from overflowing into the part of the person's emotional and physical life that does not pertain strictly to her "good works." Yet, of course, as long as the person truly fills the needs of others at her own expense, and yet is not "*too* generous," she is, no matter what her style, indisputably a good person. For we generally demand only that people *act* good (for the right reasons) to be good, and not that they reveal the appropriate sentiments in their manner and mien.

The point of sketching these types of honest and generous persons is not only to highlight a similar harshness, angularity, ungainliness, and coarseness in the two types but also to show that our current notions of "moral" and "good" apply to persons regardless of their negative "aesthetic" traits.[23] Even

---

[23] I am not at all concerned, incidentally, with whether the terms "harsh," "angular," "ungainly," "coarse," and their opposites "suave," "graceful," and "elegant," apply to such persons and their "styles" of being moral or good *metaphorically*. What *is* interesting is that they seem such appropriate terms for the circumstances.

though there appears to be no way to make persons of these two types "more moral," however, there are ways to increase their respective virtues of honesty and generosity. There is behavior that counts as "honest" behavior, even though the absence of it in a person does not make him less "moral." In addition to telling the truth and giving and taking what is due, honesty is also not speaking in conventional or bureaucratic euphemisms to refer to unpleasant truths. Honesty is not hiding your opinions and feelings behind your official position when you must do something unpleasant. Honesty is talking straight even when it is risky, risky in the emotional sense, in the sense that your masks will fall. Honesty is giving direct looks no matter what you have to say. Honesty is making warm gestures when you feel warm. Honesty is letting people know who, what, and where you are in every gesture, look, and movement. Honesty is the reverse of keeping yourself "buttoned up" and "contained" in the way you walk, and move, and hold yourself. Obviously, a person who is honest in all of these ways will also be honest in the strictly "moral" way. But he will be honest in quite a different "style" from the type described above. For since his honest behavior spills from his honest nature, his honesty is a deep-dyed trait that could not, without great effort, be prevented from showing in his behavior, and consequently it needs no constant reliance on moral principles as a fortress against its own dissolution.

Similarly, the trait of generosity can be exhibited in ways that are irrelevant to the attribution of goodness to the person. Suppose that the person caricatured above were such as to be able to "let herself go." She might then be generous with her smiles, with her tears, with friendly and endearing words, with warm gestures and reassuring touches. Such a change would, in a way, be a *bodily* change—not a change in the body's mass and shape, but in the way it moves and comports itself. One can hold oneself stiffly, tightly, and compactly, or one can unbend, yield, and "go out" in one's characteristic motions. If a person behaves in the latter sorts of ways, as well as in the "morally" generous way, her generosity will seem to permeate her very being. To call such a person "generous" is to say something deep and fundamental about her.

Honesty and generosity, thus, can be present in persons with a degree of intensity that goes far beyond what is currently considered *morally* relevant, whether the moral description is "moral" or "good." And there is excellent reason why the behavior of extreme honesty or generosity seems extra-moral under modern notions of morality. Our notions of morality presuppose the freedom to perform acts that are moral or good and to refrain from behavior that is immoral or bad. Obviously, the kind of behavior that is characteristic of extremes of honesty and generosity is located too deep within the psychic makeup of an individual to be accessible to free choice. Extreme honesty or generosity are probably not inborn, but by the time a person is old enough to be considered responsible for his own actions, it is no longer possible—simply by bending the will to the task, at least—to act in extremely honest or extremely generous ways.

Now my (pretheoretical) sense of the meaning of the term "beautiful" tells me that the term is precisely apt for describing persons of extreme honesty or generosity. It surely cannot be simply accidental that it is right to say of such persons that they carry their virtues with ease, grace, and elegance. In fact, whatever their physical endowments or lack of them, such persons also seem to carry their *bodies* with notable ease, grace, and elegance—that is, beautifully. I suspect, but do not intend to argue, that it is this connection between (morally) beautiful

91

persons and beautiful bodily movements that grounds the idea, persistent in Western culture since Plato, that a beautiful body is, or ought to be, an emblem of great virtue. Witness only Saint Bernard of Clairvaux describing the relation between beauty in the body and beauty of soul in a sermon on the *Song of Songs:*

> When this precious adornment [beauty of soul] fills the depth of the heart, then it must shine outwards like a night light hidden under a bushel, or like light shining in the darkness which cannot be hidden. Then the light, gleaming and breaking forth as it were in rays, this likeness of the mind, is taken over by the body scattered over the members and senses until every deed, speech, appearance, movement, and even laughter, acquires lustre, if it contains authority and dignity. The behaviour of these and other members and senses, their use and movement, if only it is serious, pure, modest, and without insolence and indecency, if it contains integrity and piety, will reveal the beauty of the soul, as long as there is no deceit in the spirit of this man.[24]

There are bound to be some objections that what I have described in the preceding paragraphs are not extreme degrees of the virtues of honesty and generosity, but rather some additional nonmoral virtues that are in some ways related to honesty and generosity. After all, what I have described as contributing to a high degree of honesty can also be called directness, frankness, and openness. And what I have said makes for extreme generosity can also be taken simply as friendliness, warmth, and sunniness of disposition. This objection, though, is unconvincing. True, directness, frankness, and openness are

[24] Tatarkiewicz, II, 187–88.

not the same as honesty; and friendliness, warmth, and a sunny disposition are not the same as generosity. Rather, they are like species, respectively, of honesty and generosity. For they have the same sort of relation to honesty and generosity that telling the truth, not cheating, and not stealing have to honesty and that giving money to another, working strenuously on another's behalf, and praising another have to generosity. Moreover, telling the truth is no more "like" not stealing than it is like directness and openness, and giving money to a person in need is no more "unlike" being warm and friendly to another than it is unlike praising another or working on another's behalf. Terms designating virtues like "honesty" and "generosity" simply collect fairly wide ranges of types of behavior under them.

Another objection might be that what I have described do not constitute *greater degrees* of honesty and generosity, but rather honesty or generosity in *more respects*. My first answer to this objection is that, although extreme honesty and extreme generosity are honesty and generosity in more respects, they are not *simply* that. For a crucial part of the extreme degrees of both honesty and generosity is the way in which the characteristics of honesty and generosity are possessed by people who have them in very high degree. These traits are built deep into the characters and personalities of persons having them in high degree; they are not traits that can be donned and doffed, as occasion demands, by acts of the will. Thus it is that one wants to use adverbs of degree to describe beautifully honest or generous persons; they are thoroughly, intensely, profoundly honest or generous. These adverbs convey the "saturation" of these virtues, as if they were colors.

My second answer is that at least sometimes a higher degree of some PQD in a thing is a function of the increased *number* of respects in which the PQD applies to the thing. For example, the three graces in Botticelli's "Primavera" are so very graceful because they are in graceful poses, the lines constituting their figures are graceful, their physical builds are themselves graceful, their garments are graceful and are gracefully blown by the breeze. The figures would obviously be less graceful if they were graceful in fewer respects. Thus even if extreme honesty and generosity, as I have described them, were only honesty and generosity in *more respects*, it would not at all follow that my descriptions could not be descriptions of *high degrees* of honesty and generosity.[25]

27. *Beauty and the Emotions*

There are other, nonmoral attributes of persons that are properties of qualitative degree. These are attributes of emotion, mood, and temperament: anger, sadness, joyfulness, serenity, calmness, despondency, brutality. Beauty with respect to some of these attributes is common. We have no trouble imagining a beautiful serenity or calmness come over a person, which is to say, a kind of radiant and all-encompassing serenity or calmness. One can see a beautiful joy come into a person's face, a joy that completely takes over the face, transforming it and banishing every trace of darkness. Beautiful despondency or brutality,

[25] Indeed, it is an interesting and not implausible hypothesis that all PQDs apply to their "objects" in high degree because they apply to a relatively *large number* of "respects" of those "objects." This is not the place, however, to argue for or against this hypothesis. A related hypothesis, incidentally, the pursuit of which would also be off the point right here, is that a theory of PQDs, or at least of many of them, can be constructed that is analogous to NTB, a theory that takes as its primary subject matter, not all "objects" that possess the PQDs, but all the *respects* in which "objects" possess them.

however, are impossible. The reason is that they constitute defects in a person; the despondent or brutal person has lost control. To become more and more despondent or brutal is not to become beautiful; it is to disintegrate.

Anger and sadness are much more complex. The reason they are not, in their natures, defects like despondency and brutality is that they both may be, in certain circumstances, reasonable, justifiable, and appropriate. But are extreme anger or sadness ever beautiful, and, if so, under what conditions? Part of the difficulty in answering these questions lies in trying to keep anger and sadness distinct from brutal and blind rage, and from despondency and despair. Whereas the latter tend to be, temporarily at least, all-consuming and hence disintegrating, the former cannot be such, if they are to be beautiful. Thus we must try to imagine extremes of anger and sadness that are yet in some way "controlled" so that they are not destructive of the self. Yet the "control" must not be a repression, or the proper intensity of emotion will not obtain. Clearly, what seems required to fit the concept is the anger or sadness of a special kind of person, namely, a person who is so integrated and thus so invulnerable to psychic dismantlement that neither massive anger nor profound sadness (totally appropriate to external circumstances, of course) would shatter him. What we need, in short, are persons of a godlike or heroic cast. But I have never met anyone like that. Furthermore, going into literature for examples is not generally productive, because heroes who would fit the description are not even dramatic enough to make interesting leading characters. We surely cannot take as examples of this kind of person Achilles, Agamemnon, Clytemnestra, Elektra, Odysseus, Ajax, or Medea.

What we are looking for to exemplify beautiful anger is someone who is magnificent or glorious in his wrath, much as

95

a powerful lion is magnificent and glorious in full attack de-
fending his pride. The only example of such anger that I
know, even in literature, is God's wrath. But we know that
this is such an example, not because of the descriptions given
of it, but because we can deduce that the wrath of God must
be glorious and magnificent when He sends the rebellious
angels into Hell, or when He comes to punish the wicked on
Judgment Day. The best, but I think still inadequate, example
of beautiful anger in art occurs not in literature or painting, but
in the first stanza of the "Dies Irae" in Verdi's *Requiem*. Only
compare the overpowering wrath of this music with the hysterical anger of Donna Elvira of Act I, Scene ii of *Don Giovanni* or
with the bitter, snarling anger of Elektra in the Strauss opera.
No doubt there is beauty in the latter two, yet it is not the
portrayed anger that is beautiful, but the penetration and skill
with which the composers expressed, respectively, hysterical
anger and bitter anger.[26]

Probably because of the nature of sadness and of the ability
of human beings to handle great doses of it without being

---

[26] This point raises, incidentally, a distinction in the artistic expression
of emotion that Benedetto Croce and his followers either overlook or
misdescribe. To say that beauty is expression is of course false, unless
it is taken to mean only that expression is beautiful. But the latter is
ambiguous. It could mean that *what* is expressed is beautiful and beautiful in virtue of being expressed, or it could mean that the expressing
of it is beautiful, in virtue of being a case of expressing. Now if it
means the latter, then the proposition is universally true—all expression
is beautiful—because expressing is itself an artistic achievement re-
quiring great skill and insight. It is a variety of what I called "intellectual beauty." (On the sense of "expression" I am talking about here,
see Ch. IV of my *Mind and Art*, Princeton University Press, 1972.)
But if it means the former, it is only sometimes true. For all kinds of
things that are unbeautiful in themselves, including emotion- and
mood-properties of human beings, can be expressed by an artist in
his work, like the animal passion of Clytemnestra in Aeschylus's
Agamemnon or the barbaric fury of Medea in Euripides's tragedy.

destroyed, examples of beautiful sadness are more plentiful than examples of beautiful anger. Take almost any good elegaic poem, like Milton's *Lycidas*, as an example of sadness. Take the exquisite clarinet solo expressing Andromache's sadness in the first act of Berlioz's *Les Troyens*. Take the so-called self-portrait in Michelangelo's "Pieta" in the Duomo at Florence. In these works of art there is a profound sadness that is yet beautiful because it is not desperate, but rather noble and "contained." Contrast these examples of sadness with, say, the sadness of Mary in Michelangelo's earliest "Pieta"; the latter is barely visible at all. (It is, after all, not the sadness in this work that gives it its beauty, but its dignity and tenderness, to say nothing of its material and formal properties.) Or contrast the above examples of sadness with the sadness of Michelangelo's "Rondanini Pieta," which is the sadness of helplessness and enervation. Contrast them, too, with the hysterical, if somewhat stylized, grief in the painted "Pieta" by the Master of Villeneuve in the Louvre.[27]

There is naturally much more to be said about beauty in the virtues and the emotions and many interesting cases to talk about. But I think I have said enough at least to show how beauty with respect to other virtues and other emotions might be analyzed.

28. *Sublimity*

It might occur to some that in the last two sections I have been discussing what is more properly called "sublime" than "beau-

[27] There is a color reproduction of this work in *The Fifteenth Century: From Van Eyck to Botticelli* (n.p.: Skira, 1955), p. 181.

97

tiful." As far as I can tell from reading philosophers who have famously distinguished between beauty and sublimity, the distinction is made predominantly and primarily on the basis of our characteristic reactions to, our feelings toward, the beautiful and the sublime.[28] Of course, it is also true that the kinds of "objects" that are typically beautiful differ on the whole from the kinds of "objects" that are typically sublime. Beautiful "objects" generally are small, lighthearted, joyous, charming, smiling things; sublime "objects" usually are great, grave, powerful, dark, and serious things. Because of the tendency toward subjectivism in aesthetics in the eighteenth century, it was natural then to draw distinctions between aesthetic properties in terms of our *feelings* toward them. Any single distinction drawn on this basis and hoping to be *the* basic distinction between aesthetic properties, however, can only be arbitrary.

I certainly do not want to deny the differences in our attitudes or "feelings" toward what is sublime and what is only beautiful. But merely to distinguish an attitude toward the sublime different from our attitude toward the beautiful does not entail that what is sublime, insofar as it is sublime, is not beautiful. For it probably would turn out to be true in an adequate and nuanced psychology of beauty that there is a very large class of distinguishable attitudes, reactions, or feelings, each of which is appropriate to a different kind of beautiful "object." Given the enormous variety of beautiful "objects," it is hardly conceivable that our typical "feelings" toward them all would be the same. The difference in "feeling,"

[28] See, for example, Immanuel Kant, *Observations on the Feeling of the Beautiful and Sublime*, tr. John T. Goldthwait (Berkeley: University of California Press, 1965), pp. 45–75. See also Hazard Adams (ed.), *Critical Theory Since Plato* (New York: Harcourt, Brace, 1971), pp. 310ff.

therefore, is no good reason for saying that what is sublime is not beautiful. I will argue that the sublime is in fact a species of beauty.

It is interesting to note that "objects" may possess a delicate, graceful, elegant, mysterious, sultry, or sublime beauty. And when they do, they are both beautiful and, respectively, delicate, graceful, elegant, mysterious, sultry, and sublime. Furthermore, they are, respectively, beautifully delicate, graceful, elegant, mysterious, and sultry, but *not* beautifully sublime. Now it is generally true that an "object" is beautifully F if it is beautiful with respect to F. Therefore, it seems that that which is sublimely beautiful, like the starry night, is not beautiful with respect to its sublimity, as if it were beautiful because it is so extremely sublime. "Sublimity" appears, in short, not to be a PQD.

One reason is that "sublime" already connotes an extreme degree of some sort; specifically, sublimity appears to be an extreme degree of any of a small set of PQDs, such as profundity, powerfulness, grandeur, magnificence. Thus "beautifully sublime," unlike "beautifully delicate" or "beautifully clear," is just redundant. But while "beautifully sublime" is redundant, "sublimely beautiful" is not, because "beautiful" is the more general and "sublime" the more specific term. For analogous reasons one can be joyously happy, but not happily joyous; or one's step can be ponderously heavy, but not heavily ponderous.

What the discussion so far suggests is that it is not true, as some writers on the sublime have implied, that what is sublime is not beautiful. Why sublimity is more specific than beauty, however, is not very clear. It might be so because "sublime" simply *means* "beautiful with respect to the members of some subclass of PQDs, namely, Ø." Or it might be so because "sublime" denotes a segment of the degree scale of PQDs different from, yet included in, the segment of the scale denoted by "beautiful." The latter would seem to be right, if we take seriously the analogy between "sublimely beautiful" and "joyously happy" and "ponderously heavy." If we see "happy" as denoting a high segment of the "height of spirits" scale, then "joyous" will denote the upper range of the "happiness" segment. Similarly, if "heavy" denotes the high range of a "weight" scale for steps, then "ponderous" will denote the upper range of the "heavy" segment.

In favor of this interpretation of sublimity is what happens when we try to imagine a sublime *vividness* or a sublime *delicacy*, properties that are not usually considered sublime. "Sublimely vivid" is surely what the Empyrean Rose is in Canto XXX of *Il Paradiso*, namely, a vividness that obliterates everything else in one's consciousness, which is to say, a vast and all-encompassing vividness. "Sublimely delicate," too, seems as if it might be an apt description for what is experienced when the delicacy of one's felt surroundings completely "takes over" one's consciousness so that the whole world, in all of the ways it is perceived, sensed, and understood, is reduced, as it were, to its most delicate varieties of things. Now I have not experienced any such vividness or delicacy; yet the descriptions suggest that "sublimity" attached to any beautiful property denotes an *overwhelmingly* high degree of that property.

The latter hypothesis also explains why "sublime" is attributed characteristically to "objects" of vast scale, either natural or supernatural, and attributed, furthermore, in virtue of certain sorts of vastness: vast power, vast grandeur, vast magnificence, vast glory. For it is the vastness of *scale* that increases the *degree* of powerfulness or magnificence or glory beyond the merely beautiful. It is not, then, that "sublimity" is necessarily limited to a certain small range of PQDs. It is so limited only as a matter of fact; our experience of most beautiful properties is hardly ever such that they are present in an "object" to a high enough degree to be called "sublime." Our experience with respect to properties like magnificence, glory, grandeur, powerfulness, or profundity, however, does occasionally reveal to us a degree of these properties that seems significantly higher than the extremely high degree of other properties, which seem merely to deserve the description "beautiful."[29]

29. *Harmony and Beauty*

I have talked about how NTB applies to a wide range of properties belonging to diverse categories: sensory, intellectual, artistic, moral, emotional. But I have said nothing about harmony, that is, about the beauty things might have because of the way their elements are related. Traditionally harmony has loomed very large in discussions of beauty. Some artists and philosophers have wanted to identify beauty with harmony. Nearly everyone—hedonists like Santayana and expression-theorists like Croce are exceptions—has made "harmony" or some closely related concept at least a part of his theory of beauty. I believe that "harmony" should not so figure in a *theory* of the beautiful, but I acknowledge that harmony is an important part of the *subject matter* of a theory of beauty. Thus, although harmony does deserve the attention it has received

[29] Since first writing this section I have read that, at least according to E. F. Carritt in *The Theory of Beauty* (London: Methuen, 1962), pp. 149–76, the concept of sublimity has often in the literature on the subject meant a very high degree of beauty.

in traditional aesthetics, it does not deserve the privileged position it was accorded by so much of that tradition.

Beautiful "objects" are often beautiful because of the harmony among their parts, and probably more "objects" are beautiful because of their harmony than are beautiful because of any other single property. Moreover, an extremely wide variety of "objects"—landscapes, color combinations, spatial configurations of all sorts, human and animal bodies, paintings, musical compositions, and personalities—can be harmonious. Any "object" that has elements that can relate to one another can be harmonious; and "element" can range over just as broad a domain as "object" can. "Harmony" seems, in fact, unlike other beautiful properties, to be just as widely applicable as "beautiful" itself. It is no wonder that traditional aestheticians were impressed by the phenomenon of harmony.

Naturally the term "harmony" has not always meant the same to everyone who has used it. I take the term in the fairly vague sense of "the going together of elements" that it possesses in such ordinary, everyday use as it has. Although "harmony" is vague, however, it is surely no vaguer than other PQDs, which are, as a class, an eminently vague lot. For harmony is clearly a PQD: colors can *go together very well;* building styles can *just barely go together* without clashing; shrubs in a garden can *go all right together*, but not do anything special for one another. There are, in short, degrees of harmony. Beauty with respect to harmony, as with other PQDs, is an extremely high degree of it.

I do not intend to set forth a theory of harmony here. Nor am I obliged to do so, any more than I am obliged to set forth a theory of any other beautiful properties. What makes certain combinations of elements more or less harmonious is certainly as interesting a question as (but no more interesting than) what makes things graceful, or solid-looking, or craggy, or serene. And there probably is as much, or as little, hope of discovering a general theory of harmony as there is of discovering a general theory of many other beautiful properties. One should recognize, however, that harmony, like other beautiful properties, is relative to the sort of elements that are in harmony. Harmony of color is not harmony of lines, or actions, or styles; and judgments of harmonious beauty must be made with this fact in mind. There is no way, for example, of deciding which "go better together" and, therefore, which are more beautiful: the colors in this tie or the buildings around the Main Square. And, as with other PQDs, the fact that there is no way of answering this question does not mean that the harmony among the colors and the harmony among the buildings are very, very "close" in degree, but rather that the two harmonies are simpy not comparable.

There are some conditions of harmony that deserve consideration here. One is that harmony obtains only among elements that are themselves beautiful. There can be no architectural harmony among dilapidated, nondescript, and ugly buildings, nor can there be color harmony among dulled, faded, or muddy colors. This does not mean, of course, that there can be no color harmony among muted colors like those of the California chaparral country. For colors like the latter can be (color-relatively) vivid, even though they are not bright hues.

But simply putting beautiful elements together is not sufficient to create harmony among them. I can hardly imagine a less harmonious urban scene than St. Peter's Cathedral, Chartres Cathedral, the Taj Mahal, the Seagram Building, and the Temple of Neptune at Paestum all arranged around a gigantic plaza with the Washington Monument in its center. For in such an arrangement the separate beauties of all the elements would compete with rather than complement one another. In an harmonious arrangement the elements must all be "keyed" to one another so that each will contribute to the beauty of the other and hence to the beauty of the whole. The colors of a chaparral forest are thus "keyed" to one another; it is as if a brown wash had uniformly been applied to the greens, reds, and golds. It is the lack of a uniform key that makes the combination of a bright Chinese red shirt and a frosted green jacket inharmonious. For the jacket makes the shirt color look garish and the shirt makes the jacket color look drab. But if the shirt is a frosted red and thus is keyed to the frosted green of the jacket, the red and the green, being complementary, will accentuate each other to produce a harmonious color combination.

An interesting implication of the necessity of "keying" in harmonious combinations is that sometimes ugliness, or at least the absence of beauty, can be a result of beauty. This happens if an element, beautiful in some respects, is put in combinations to which it is not "keyed." Thus a massive, powerful-looking, greatly dynamic, but gracefully bending freeway interchange may be stunningly beautiful situated in some austere, rocky foothills that neither dwarf nor are dwarfed by the concrete masses of the freeway. But situated in—or over—a comfortable, tree-shrouded residential neighborhood that it dominates by its scale, the same freeway interchange becomes obscene and ugly. What happens in the latter situation is that the interchange acquires properties like coarseness and brutal aggressiveness.

Coarseness and brutal aggressiveness in persons are of course defects, and although the properties of the freeway interchange are not just like the properties of persons denoted by the same words, the use of the same words to describe the interchange does show that the properties of the freeway are not beautiful properties. Yet it seems clear that the properties of coarseness or brutal aggressiveness are not defects, lacks, or deficiencies of freeways. A reasonable interpretation of "coarse" and "brutally aggressive" when applied to freeways, however, is "coarse-looking" or "aggressive-seeming," in which the suffixes of "appearance" make explicit the metaphorical use of "coarse" and "aggressive" applied to freeways. Thus we may think of "coarse" and "aggressive" when applied to a freeway as signifying the "appearance" of defects; and, as such, they are not beautiful properties. They are, if anything, "ugly properties." In this case, then, the particular beauties of the freeway result in its own ugliness, as well as the ugliness of the total environment it is in, when it is introduced into a setting to which it is not "keyed."

A similar phenomenon occurs when a fluorescent green "No Smoking" sign comes into view while you are hiking through the chaparral forest. The green of the sign is, of course, extremely vivid and beautiful in that respect. Nevertheless, with that fluorescent green occupying a significant portion of your visual field, the surrounding forest, which can in no way compete in brightness with the sign, becomes dull- and drab-looking. And the color of the sign, when you step far enough away from it, although it loses not very much of its vividness, acquires other, anthropomorphic properties like "obtrusiveness" and "rudeness" because it (1) spoils the beauty of the forest by drabbing it out and (2) upsets the harmony of the total visual scene. Thus it is that the very vividness of the sign (that is, its beauty) is the cause of the disharmony and drabness (that is, the lack of beauty) in its surroundings. Now although in this particular sort of situation, it is the artificial green sign that is the culprit, in other situations the natural coloration of the chaparral could be the ugly-making factor. Imagine, for instance, a small photograph of typical chaparral scenery being placed on a large painting of brilliant "electric" hues. In such a context it would be the natural colors that obtrude themselves and cause the disharmony.

Interestingly, disharmony can even be caused by putting together beautiful elements that are beautiful with respect to the "same" properties. The metal towers that support power lines are often regarded as ugly, but they are not necessarily so. In fact, when a line of them is strung out over the low, grassy, rounded hills south of here and they are seen in the evening silhouetted against the western sky, they look like elegant giantesses in long flimsy dresses strolling over the sturdy hills—delicate figures on their own scale. When the many articulations of the metal structures are highlighted by being shown off against the sky, the towers take on a surprising but beautiful delicacy. But think of driving through a greatly delicate spring landscape of puffy white clouds, mistily blue hills in the distance, fresh green grass, and just-leafing trees. And imagine one of these towers suddenly looming up in your visual field. Probably the tower will spoil the delicacy of the scene for you. That is likely to be so even if you imagine the tower as being somehow in shadow so that its form appears clearly articulated against the natural setting. Such experiences occur fairly often, and that is why we tend to think of such towers as ugly "in themselves." But how can the "delicate" structure spoil the "delicate" natural scene? It does so because the delicacy of the former is the delicacy of gigantic, hard, geometrically shaped metal constructions, whereas the delicacy of the latter is that of grass, trees, mists, and clouds. They are therefore no more "keyed" together than the Chinese red shirt and the frosted green jacket, which are both vivid (color-relatively speaking). But just as the brightness of the red drabs out the frosted green, obscuring the latter's color-relative vividness, the delicacy of mists and fresh green sprouts hardens and stiffens the geometric filigree of the tower and obscures its (peculiar kind of) delicacy. In this situation, ironically, although it is the tower that seems to be the intruder and the destroyer of beauty, it is actually the delicacies of the natural scene that obscure the peculiar delicacy of the tower by highlighting the very properties of the tower that do not harmonize with the landscape.

30. The "Flowers of Evil" Phenomenon

What the preceding discussion shows is that disharmony—either the lack of beauty or ugliness—can be an effect of beauty. There are several other interesting kinds of phenomena, related to the above, the possibility of which is deducible from NTB. It can happen, for instance, that an "object's" property, beautiful in itself, results in that "object's" being unbeautiful or even repulsively ugly. As a child I received as an Easter gift two live chicks whose feathers had been dyed glowingly beautiful colors, one orange and the other purple. Although the colors were undoubtedly beautiful, with a type of beauty appealing especially to children, the chicks were, even to my mind then, and even more to my mind now, sad and grotesque creatures. They gave me nightmares for weeks. A similar phenomenon occurs when edible items are bathed, as sometimes at parties, in vivid colored light that, though beautiful in itself, can make the food appear anything but beautiful. Similarly, vivid green light will make human faces look ghoulish and red light will make them look evil. And yet what prompts people to use such lighting, when ugly effects are not intended, is precisely the beauty of colored light.

It is also true that "objects" that are, for a variety of reasons, repulsive and definitely not beautiful may naturally, and not just by artifice, possess properties that are, in that very instantiation, beautiful. The motion of the mushroom cloud of an atomic bomb explosion has a kind of sublime grace, and its billowing, vaporous volume is beautifully voluptuous-looking. Yet it is hard, because of its moral obscenity, to call the explosion itself beautiful. A fresh, gaping wound will produce a profusion of gorgeously vivid blood. A rupture in a slug's skin can produce a gracefully swelling mound of beautifully smooth, creamy-white guts. Or, as Baudelaire saw in the corpse by the roadside, there is a beauty in the sensuously pulsing rhythm of the flies as they swarm up and down over the putrid vulva.

We can even go further and find properties that make up the very essence, as it were, of sickness, deformity, and decay but that are nevertheless beautiful. Even the dark amethyst color of a bruise on a human limb can be beautiful, though the bruise is not beautiful. A pine tree's needles, ugly when killed by the smog, can show brilliantly bronze in the sun and thus harbor beauty in the very color of death. The lacy skeleton of a dead oak tree against the sky can be lovely. And a genius like Baudelaire can find even in putrescence itself the "blooming richness," as of a flower's, when he scrutinizes a rotting corpse and sees it actually and potentially teeming with life—the life of flies and maggots. For obvious reasons we can appropriately call the sort of beauty described in this section the "Flowers of Evil" phenomenon.[30]

[30] I don't claim that Baudelaire meant by his title only what I mean here, though I think he did have such phenomena in mind. Surely his

There is a subtle problem raised by these kinds of phenomena, namely, how exactly to *locate* the beauty. It is clear that the "primary 'object' " in all the examples is not beautiful (*simpliciter*). That is, the food, the chicks, the explosion, the wound, the slug, the corpse are not beautiful. But, more troublesomely, it seems not even to be true that they are *beautiful with respect to* the "beautiful properties" they instantiate. Yet NTB says that beautiful properties are such only insofar as they are present in an "object" to a high degree. The solution to this problem is relatively simple: we attribute the beautiful properties in these cases, not to the "primary 'objects'," but to "secondary 'objects'." Thus it is the *color* of the chicks, the *light* on the food, the *motion* of the explosion's mushroom cloud, the *blood* of the wound, the *guts* of the slug, the *swarming* of the flies on the corpse that instantiate the respective beautiful properties.

A related problem is the following. Rustiness in a hand saw is a defect and therefore, according to NTB, no saw can be beautiful with respect to that property. And yet it is easily imaginable that we come across an old saw that, having been buried for years in damp ground, shows such interesting texture and color precisely because it is extremely rusty. In such a case it is conceivable that we would want to call the saw beautiful precisely with respect to its extreme rustiness. Yet NTB does not allow us to call it thus. Is this a counterexample to NTB? The answer is not simple, but it is ultimately no. For the beauty of the saw with respect to the rustiness can be redescribed in such a way as to fit the requirements of NTB. Thus it may be the "depthy" crustiness of the *rust* on the saw, or the harmonious medley of the colors of the *rust*, that makes the rustiness of the saw beautiful. That is, we change "rustiness" to

---

title also refers to the beauty of the poetry that he wrote about "evil" subject matters.

"rust," and rust then becomes the unproblematically beautiful "object," beautiful with respect to its crustiness of texture and harmony of color. By this maneuver NTB can comprehend all of the beauty in a high degree of a property of defect. I see no reason, moreover, why such a maneuver would not take care of all analogous cases.

This maneuverability of NTB shows in another way how NTB is a general theory of beauty but not a general theory of uses of the term "beautiful." For in cases like the rusty saw NTB cannot sanction what is clearly a legitimate use of "beautiful," and yet it is able to comprehend all of the beauty that exists in the rusty saw. In fact, it is an outstanding virtue of NTB that it can account for the whole gamut of "Flowers of Evil" phenomena. NTB is thus able to integrate the ancient insight that beauty cannot range over the damaged, the decayed, the defective, and the deformed with the distinctively modern discovery that beauty can bloom in the very anus of ugliness.

31. *Disagreements about Beauty*

Part of the argument strategy I have used in this essay has been to exhibit the power of NTB by showing how it applies to a diverse variety of *prima facie* unassimilable cases of beauty. At the same time I have been able partially to justify several recurrent themes in the tradition of speculation about beauty. The themes are: (1) the close link between beauty and goodness, (2) the connection between "utility" and beauty, (3) the application of beauty to moral character, (4) the intimate connection between harmony and beauty. What I mean when I say that NTB has "justified" these themes is that NTB can not only show that the *intuitions* behind these themes were sound but also suggest what is correct (and incorrect) in traditional *theories* based on those intuitions.

Another test of a theory of beauty is how it accounts for disagreements between judgments of beauty. "Accounting for disagreements" means at least two things. First, a good theory must be able to explain plausibly the obvious fact that judgments of beauty diverge significantly from person to person and from culture to culture. Second, a good theory must be able to describe accurately the conditions under which disagreements have been satisfactorily resolved and to prescribe ways in which future disagreements can be satisfactorily resolved. Thus the value of NTB, as of most theories, depends in part on its future usefulness.

In order to explain disagreements in judgments of beauty in terms of NTB we must keep in mind (1) that there are an indefinitely large number of PQDs and (2) that this number is multiplied by the "relativity" of all PQDs applying to more than one sort of "object." This relativity means that even "objects" that are judged beautiful (*simpliciter*) are certain to be less than beautiful with respect to some PQDs. For example, a thoroughbred horse that is beautiful (*simpliciter*) will not be beautiful—will be the very opposite—with respect to luxuriant furriness of coat. In fact, for most beautiful "objects," the very existence of beauty with respect to one PQD will preclude beauty with respect to another. In the case of the beautiful thoroughbred, its extreme sleekness guarantees that it will lack luxuriance in its coat.

Another salient fact is that some PQDs, and perhaps most of them, are uncommon in the sense of being rarely encountered. Sometimes it seems, in fact, that the most delightfully beautiful properties are encountered only once—the explosive look of my eucalyptus tree, for example, or the "sparkling" quality of the delicate dried weeds with the sharp-looking seed pods I saw this morning highlighted against some dark earth.[31]

Another fact about PQDs is that, often in virtue of their rarity, they may be difficult to describe. This explains why PQDs are frequently described in metaphors that are non-standard. It often happens that we are forced, in accounting for perceived beauty, to cast about for a proper description and finally to give one in terms of metaphors we invent just for that case. Metaphors can be more or less apt, and it takes a special talent to contrive new and apt metaphors for rare experiences. The more apt a metaphor, of course, the greater the chance is that the experience described thereby can be communicated to others. One of the talents good critics of the arts must have is the ability to describe new PQDs they have encountered in seeing, hearing, or reading unfamiliar art.

Yet another fact about PQDs is that since they almost always are applicable to an "object" relative to one *sort* of "object" among many sorts, and since what is a high degree of a PQD often depends crucially on which sort of object it is being applied relative to, the ability to perceive that a given "object" is beautiful with respect to a PQD depends upon being reasonably familiar with "objects" of that sort. This fact explains in part why we often cannot evaluate a piece of art until we have seen at least several pieces "like" it—either in the same style or by the same artist.

Finally, the fact that, according to NTB, beauty is a high degree of a PQD means that two or more persons using this

---

[31] Of course, it cannot be true that the occasion on which we perceive a beautiful property as beautiful is in fact the only occasion when we have encountered it. For, as I pointed out earlier, it takes experience of a range of instances of a property before we are able to judge the property's presence in an extremely high degree.

concept of beauty with respect to the same PQD can come to different judgments if they have experienced a different range of instances of that PQD. Suppose that person A has experience of these instances of F—a, b, c, d, e, f—which he ranks in just that order with f being beautiful and everything from d on down being unbeautiful. But suppose that person B has experience only of a, b, c, d. B may then justifiably call d beautiful with respect to F, while A may justifiably call d unbeautiful.

Now what these five facts together imply is that the probability, intuitively speaking, of widespread disagreement in judging beauty is very high. For to agree that an "object" X that is not a PQD is either beautiful of unbeautiful (*simpliciter*), two persons would have to be counting, out of a large class of PQDs applicable to X, roughly the same PQDs as relevant to X's beauty and roughly the same PQDs as not relevant to X's beauty. In order to do this the two must perceive at least the PQDs of X that count in favor of its beauty. But to do that they must both perceive what may be a fairly rare property, which (1) may have no standard description in their language and (2) which may well be very difficult for either of the two to describe aptly. And even if they both perceive the relevant PQDs, they must both have had experience of a sufficiently large number of instances of those PQDs, and the instances of each PQD that each person experienced must have exhibited the same range of degrees. Given what we can assume generally about the wide variances of perceptual and linguistic abilities among people and what we know about the different experiences of people, especially from culture to culture and especially with respect to art, a realm where beauty is characteristically relevant, it comes to seem almost miraculous that there exists as much agreement in judgments of beauty as there does.

To describe how disagreements are resolved and resolvable

under NTB, let us set up schematically several types of disagreements:

1. A and B disagree about whether X, an "object" but not a PQD, is beautiful (*simpliciter*).
2. A and B disagree about whether an instance of F, a PQD, is beautiful or, what is the same, A and B disagree about whether X is beautiful with respect to F.
3. A and B disagree about whether X is beautiful (*simpliciter*) but agree that X is beautiful with respect to F, G, H, . . . , N and is not beautiful with respect to P, Q, R, . . . , N.

The persons having a type 1 disagreement should first discover those respects in which A thinks X is beautiful and B thinks X is not beautiful. These circumstances are then possible:

1.1 A and B agree about the properties making X beautiful and making X not beautiful and

    1.11 may still disagree about whether X is beautiful (*simpliciter*) or not, in which case the disagreement turns into one of type (3), or

    1.12 may then agree either that X is beautiful or that X is not beautiful, or

    1.13 may then agree that there is no point to the argument about X being beautiful (*simpliciter*), that the best judgment is that X is beautiful with respect to F, G, and H and not beautiful with respect to P, Q, and R.

1.2 A and B agree about the beauty of all the beauty-making properties and about the nonbeauty of all the nonbeauty-making properties except F, which A calls beautiful and B not beautiful. The disagreement thus turns out to be one of type 2.

1.3   A and B agree about the beauty of all the beauty-making properties and about the nonbeauty of all the nonbeauty-making properties, except F. A says that X does not possess F, and B says that X does. Resolving a dispute like this is not the business of NTB. For that we need a theory of F. Persons who think it a pity that I do not offer a theory of PQDs or a theory of "aesthetic qualities" (which are surely all PQD's) in this essay should at least thank NTB for revealing some of the importance of the class of PQDs and for giving an interesting reason why "aesthetic qualities" are aesthetic.[32]

Persons having a disagreement of type 2 should compare their experiences of F to see whether they have both experienced the same "objects" possessing F. These are then the possibilities:

2.1   A and B have the same experiences of "objects" with F; however, they do not agree that the instant case is a case of F in an extremely high degree. NTB cannot provide a resolution of this disagreement, which is the job of a theory of F or of a general theory of "high degree" in PQDs.

[32] Of course, not all PQDs are what most aestheticians these days want to call "aesthetic qualities." NTB, however, at least *suggests* that the notion of aesthetic quality limited to anything less than the whole class of PQDs is arbitrary. The fact that nearly everybody now thinks that the class of aesthetic qualities is so limited stems from the deep modern prejudice that the aesthetic is radically different from the moral, the utilitarian, and the intellectual. And this prejudice stems in large part from Kant. But, as I suggested earlier, since Kant's separation of free beauty from adherent beauty is ill-grounded, so is the modern prejudice stemming therefrom.

2.2 A and B do not have the same experiences of "objects" with *F*, in which case

    2.21 they take steps to equalize their experiences with respect to *F* so that

        2.211) they resolve this disagreement, or

        2.212) the disagreement is of type (2.1); or

    2.22 they cannot equalize their experiences with respect to *F* so that the argument is unresolvable through no fault of NTB.

Persons having a disagreement of type 3 can get no help from NTB at all in resolving the disagreement, because NTB specifies no sufficient conditions for an "object" being beautiful (*simpliciter*). One effect of my argument that NTB is a comprehensive theory of beauty, in the sense that there is no beauty that eludes its grasp, is to show either that there is no point to disagreements of type 3 or that whatever point they have has nothing to do with the presence or absence of any property of *X*, but perhaps has to do with the expression of certain preferences or biases of A and B. Therefore, the effect of NTB on disagreements of type 3 is not to *resolve*, but to *dissolve* them.

Of actual disagreements about beauty I suspect that most belong to type 1 and that 1.13 is the resolution most people should come to and will eventually come to. I think 1.3 is the second most likely type of resolution, which of course just raises another kind of disagreement. In the absence of a theory for each PQD or of a general theory of them all, we rely for resolution of such disagreements on the kind of discourse we use to get other people to see the same properties that we do. Art criticism is simply a more developed and systematic form of such discourse, specifically relevant to getting people to perceive beauty (and other things) in the arts. Probably the next most frequent kind of disagreement is type 2.2. In short, NTB implies that most genuine disputes in judgments of beauty are due either to the failure of the disputants to reveal the grounds of their judgments, a lack of perceptiveness or sensitivity in one of the disputants, or the disparity of the experiences of the disputants with regard to the sort of "object" under discussion.

I want to be very clear, however, that NTB does not claim to be able to rationalize all discourse using the term "beautiful." There might still remain, after NTB has done its work, all those judgments that some "object" is beautiful (*simpliciter*). Whether one calls an object X beautiful or refuses to do so, even after agreeing on those respects in which X is beautiful, may very well be due to the different sorts of properties one especially prizes, whether such preferences are purely personal or exemplify some general social or cultural attitudes. Indeed, it is this logical possibility that grounds the possibility of a historical or sociological study of aesthetic preferences. In other words, far from being incompatible with a history or sociology of "taste," NTB is able to pinpoint exactly what the subject matter of such an enterprise ought to be. The success of NTB also indirectly demonstrates the fallacy of the common, but usually implicit, inference that, because there so obviously is a history of taste, beauty is not objective.

32. *The Limited Use of "Beautiful"*

One of the standard "arguments" used in this century against devoting philosophical energy to questions of beauty is that the terms "beautiful" and "beauty" are "hardly ever used." Now the premise of the argument can hardly be disputed; "beauty," it is true, does not have a very rich or very large role to play in the language either of contemporary critics of the arts or of ordinary mortals. Far from indicating the unimportance of beauty, however, this fact is readily explainable by a true theory of beauty.

Outside of philosophical discussions "beautiful" occurs chiefly in simple declarative sentences or, more often, in exclamations: "How beautiful!" "Look how beautiful!" Sentences in which "beautiful" is used either have the form or imply (not necessarily strictly) sentences of the form X *is beautiful*. These expressions have, generally speaking, three functions other than the one of referring to something beautiful. (1) They may be purely spontaneous expressions of delight; (2) they may function as a compliment to someone, as when we appreciate our host's etchings, his scotch, or his sofa; or (3) they may be uttered in order to get a companion to share our experience of a sight or a sound.

Obviously, these are not exclusive functions, nor is the list exhaustive. Since these are the major functions of expressions using "beautiful," however, it is fairly clear why the term is "hardly ever used." Beauties are rather plentiful, and if one were to exclaim over each one out loud "Oh, how beautiful!" or some such, one would either (1) talk to oneself a lot, (2) interrupt other people quite a bit, or (3) sound more effusive than most people are, or want to seem. The result is that exclamations (or judgments) of beauty of the first sort are generally made to oneself. The infrequency of the second use of "beautiful" follows from the very fact that the use is appropriate only on specialized, quasi-ceremonial occasions. Neither of these uses requires or generally receives follow-up conversation in which "beauty" figures prominently.

The third use is more interesting. Suppose you suddenly notice something that strikes you as remarkably beautiful and you want your companion to share the experience. If the something either is obviously beautiful or has a beauty that you can presume will be obvious to your companion, it is not even necessary to use the term "beautiful." "Oh look!" or "Wow!" or "Get those hills!" or a nudge and a pointed finger will do the job. On the other hand, if what you see or hear would not be obvious to your companion (like the subtle way the red roofs bring out the red tints in the surrounding hills or the exquisitely lacy-looking weed four paces to the right in a field of a million weeds), you are likely not to try to get your companion to share the experience. For if the experience is to be shared, your companion will have to see exactly what you see. But to get him to see just right might call for a lot of analysis, precise description, and some discussion. It is this very sort of verbal activity, however, that most people either cannot engage in or cannot engage in well. It is sometimes those persons most sensitive to subtle and hard-to-find beauties who are either least capable of such analyses or least willing, by virtue of temperament or "ideology," to enter into such activity.

Even for persons who can fairly easily engage in this analytical activity, it is more than likely (1) to ruin their own experience and (2) to fail to arouse the same experience in the other. The beauties that we commonly encounter are often so fleeting that most people do not want to risk spoiling the experience of them by discussing them. And we all, doubtless, have had the frustrating experience of never quite getting someone else to notice what we noticed. Even in museums and during the intermissions at concerts, where the environment is ideal for pedantry and snobbishness to flourish, analyses and discussions of specific beauties seem stilted and pointless to all but the most determined of pedants and snobs. Thus we see why it is that reasonable (and reasonably noncompulsive) people "hardly ever" use the term "beautiful."

We can also see why critics of the arts hardly ever use the term "beautiful" even when discussing arts that are, and are intended to be, beautiful. In the first place, art works are generally very complex, each one exhibiting many, and many different kinds of, properties. Thus simply calling a work beautiful would not, by itself, be useful. We would still want to know in virtue of what it is beautiful. And if it is presumed we know in advance the respects in which it is beautiful, there is no point to the critical remark at all. Yet, if the critic does point out the varieties of properties that make the work beautiful, that description alone is sufficient. He need not, and therefore usually does not, go on and say that the work is beautiful. The reason is that if his readers apprehend the great degree of skill, inventiveness, wit, harmony, expressiveness, or whatever that the work exhibits, they already apprehend its beauties.

A related reason that critics in the twentieth century do not use the term "beautiful" is that, confronted as we are with a wealth of extraordinarily diverse art—of past styles, of foreign styles, of idiosyncratic contemporary styles—the term "beautiful" applied to a piece of art is especially uninformative and unhelpful. What we want the critics to do, not always but often, is to describe for us the special and important properties of each kind of art. We frequently must be taught what to look or listen for in each kind. When we know that, and are reasonably adept at spotting those properties, the specific beauties of each kind of art need no special discovery; they will exist, like all beauties, wherever an extremely high degree of those properties exists. That is a reason why the best critical work, when it is concerned with beauty,[33] will mention beauty seldom, if at all.

[33] I don't want to give the impression that all criticism of the arts is concerned with specific beauties of its objects, for it is not. Some

I have listed only the good reasons why critics in this century would not use the term "beautiful" very much. There are obvious bad ones: the critic may be afraid to use a term that is so unfashionable, or he may believe a false theory of beauty and therefore not know he is talking about beauty. The bad reasons may in fact be the ones that are operative most of the time. I have tried to point out, nevertheless, that there are perfectly good reasons for not using "beautiful" very much, and that they have nothing to do with the notion that beauty is an inappropriate or a nonexistent subject matter for philosophers.

33. *The Objectivity of Beauty*

My argument for NTB is concluded. It is time to say a little something in answer to a question that is apparently unavoidable in any discussion of beauty: Is beauty objective or subjective? The difficulty in getting a clear answer to this question has always been a function of (1) the difficulty in determining what beauty is and (2) the difficulty in determining what the subjective-objective distinction amounts to. Thus, even if we are content with NTB, the second difficulty still looms large. This difficulty specifically is that there are several standard

---

criticism tries to specify the "effect" the art has on us when we view, hear, or read it. Some criticism tries to "place" the art in its time, or in the history of that art, or to talk about its ideational content. Some critical talk, furthermore, is occupied only with aspects of technique or narrowly with the particular artistic means employed in the art.

On the other hand, criticism that describes formal or sensuous properties in a work, or discovers "intellectual" properties in a work, such as wit, imagination, skill, inventiveness, or describes and evaluates the attitudes, temperaments, sensibilities, characters, or personalities revealed in the art—such criticism is concerned with beauty whether the critic knows it or not.

meanings of "subjective" and "objective" used by both philosophers and nonphilosophers, and none of them is especially
clear. All, or several, of these meanings may be related in various
intricate ways, but they are not obviously so. *Prima facie*,
therefore, "objective" and "subjective" are highly ambiguous.
One virtue of NTB is that, specifying at last what beauty is,
it allows us to choose our favorite meaning of "subjective"
and "objective" and answer the "unavoidable" question about
beauty.

I do not intend to explore that question thoroughly, for to
do so would involve a systematic treatment of all the plausible
or important senses of "subjective" and "objective," a treatment that would be too tedious both to write and to read. I
have no doubt that there are senses of "subjective" in which
beauty, as understood by NTB, would turn out to be subjective.
I suspect, however, that very much else would turn out to
be subjective on those criteria, too. Also, because beauty is a
function of properties belonging to a certain broad class, there
might well be meanings of "subjective" and "objective" according to which some beauty would be subjective and some
would be objective. In the next few pages I intend to explain
how and why beauty, as determined by NTB, is objective in a
sense that is important at least in the history of modern speculations about beauty.

In the discussion of vividness I noted that the color of a
thing will appear more or less vivid under differing conditions,
but that this sense of "appear," instead of contrasting with
"really be," is interchangeable with it. The same point can be
made with respect to most other beautiful properties. Without
ice the taste of scotch seems (and is) smoother than with ice.
A pattern of foliage appears (and is) more lacy-looking against
the sky than against the darker and more variegated backdrop

of mountains. A musical passage may sound (and be) sadder when played on a violin than when played on a piano. The figure of the bull may appear (and be) more solid-looking against the golden grass than against the dark green trees.[34]

What this fact means is that, however much beauty is appearance, it is not illusion. Some people have thought that the subjective is that which, like the illusory, has no just claim to reality. On this view of subjectivity, of course, beauty as it is understood by NTB is not subjective. But it is also true, on such a view of subjectivity, that such things as pains, pleasures, feelings of depression and elation, joys, and sorrows can be, because they are not necessarily illusory, objective. Such a consequence does not disturb me, but it would others. For to many, sensations, feelings, and emotions are paradigmatic of the subjective.

As a matter of fact, it was near the end of the eighteenth century, after many attempts to find criteria of beauty among the properties of beautiful things failed, that the notion that beauty is subjective in the latter sense took hold.[35] Kant exemplifies this trend in declaring that the judgment of beauty is not determined by concepts but by a feeling of the subject. It is not absolutely clear from the Kantian texts, but it is nowhere denied in them, that Kant means to say that a certain feeling a person has is *sufficient* ground for him to judge whatever produces it to be beautiful. On this criterion of "subjective," too, beauty as determined by NTB is objective. For

[34] Not all beautiful properties will bear this sense of "appear." The moral beauty of a person does not depend upon temporary and occasional circumstances, but upon the inner nature of the person. Therefore, if it is ever proper to say of a person in some circumstance that he appears morally beautiful, that must mean either (1) that it is not certain whether he really is morally beautiful or (2) that it is not really the case that he is such. The same goes for cases of "functional" beauty, such as being beautiful for making masts or weaving baskets.

[35] Stolnitz, *op. cit.*

although it is true, as I argued before, that a *necessary* condition of one's legitimately judging something as beautiful is that he take pleasure (or some comparable positive feeling) in apprehending it, such pleasure is not *sufficient* ground for such a judgment. Rather, the existence of beauty in a property of a thing depends upon the degree to which that property is present in the thing.

We can bring out this sort of objectivity in a new way by showing how beautiful properties, that is, PQDs, are unlike the "property" of being pleasant. We can, in fact, distinguish PQDs from a whole class of properties like *being pleasant*, such as *being painful, delightful, disgusting, enjoyable, exhilarating, depressing, desirable, repulsive*. These all belong to a class of properties that implicity indicate the *effect* of an "object" possessing it on a person who apprehends it. I will call them "PSEs," short for "properties of psychological effect."

The interesting thing about PSEs is that they seem, *prima facie*, to be PQDs. One "object" can surely be *more* pleasant, painful, depressing, exhilarating than another, and the differences in degree are not enumerable on a scale that applies generally to all "objects" possessing a single PSE. Despite these similarities, however, PSEs are not PQDs. For their true form is hidden by the suffixes *ing, ive, ful, able*. (The *ant* suffix in *pleasant* comes directly from the French, in which *ant* suffixes indicate the present participle.) And what these suffixes in general mean is that what is signified by the stem of the word is a kind of "effect." Thus "pleasant" means something like "giving pleasure"; "painful" means "causing pain"; "delightful" means "yielding delight"; "desirable" means "arousing desire"; and so forth.

We can understand how PSEs fit into the sentential form X *is* F by construing the suffixes of standard PSE words as "causative of." Thus "pleasant" becomes "causative of pleasure," "enjoyable" becomes "causative of enjoyment," and so on. This interpretation will give all PSEs a uniform form as well as revealing how they can be understood as properties under our earlier interpretation of "property." Once PSEs are put into this form, it becomes obvious that the degrees of a PSE do not apply to the property as a whole, but only to the "effect." The form of "more pleasant" is shown to be "causative of more pleasure"; the form of "less delightful" is "causative of delight"; the form of "more enjoyable" is "causative of more enjoyment." In this respect PSEs are shown to be only superficially like PQDs and ultimately distinct from them.

One might say, in objection, that some genuine PQD's also take forms other than their apparent ones. For example, properties of the (apparent) form *being F-looking* can also take the form *having a look of F-ness*.[36] But notice that *more F-looking* translates into *has more of a look of F-ness*, not into *has a look of more F-ness*, as it would have to if a true analogy were to hold between PSEs and PQDs of the form *being F-looking*.

The reason for the above is that *is F-looking* does not translate as *looks F*. The bull that is more solid-looking in the golden grass than against the trees does not look solider there; he looks just as solid in either place. To say that he looks less solid against the tree suggests that he looks as if, when you pressed him, he would feel a bit squishy and jelly-like and

---

[36] Strictly speaking, anything of this form is not a property because it cannot be fitted into a sentence-beginning of the form X *is* . . . . But this fact does not affect the importance of my hypothetical objection. For any sentence of the form X *is F* can be translated into one of the form X *has F-ness* or an obvious variant. Thus X *is F-looking* could just as well be X *has F-lookingness*, in which case X *has a look of F-ness* would appear to relate to it very much as X *has the effect of delight* relates to X *has delightfulness*.

thus quite unlike most bulls, whereas to say that he is less solid-looking is merely to say that he gives no especially vivid impression or appearance of solidity. Generally, to say something of the form *X looks F* is a way to express doubt or agnosticism about *X*'s really being *F*. But, generally, to say something of the form *X is F-looking* is not to express doubt or to withhold judgment about a property of *X*, but is to assert something definite about *X*, namely, that *X* presents a certain appearance.

Such being the case, then, the form *X is more F-looking* translates into the form *X has more of a look of F-ness*, which is analogous to *X has more elegance* (from *X is more elegant*) and *X has more honesty* (from *X is more honest*). It is not analogous to *X is causative of more pleasure* (from *X is more pleasant*) or *X is causative of more depression* (from *X is more depressing*). Thus, in setting up its criterion of beauty as applicable primarily to certain properties of "objects," NTB appeals to no PSEs, nor does it include them in its subject matter. Even more importantly, however, the class of properties that have traditionally been the chief weapons of subjectivist theories of beauty is thereby, as a class, distinguishable from the cornerstone of NTB, the class of PQDs. I have no doubt that most serious theorists of beauty in the whole Western tradition, both objectivists and subjectivists, would think of NTB as an objectivist theory.

34. *The Problem of the Enjoyment of Beauty*

A subjectivist theory of beauty that says that beauty is identical with what pleases, delights, or otherwise causes enjoyment has absolutely no difficulty in explaining our enjoyment of beauty.

In fact, the problem does not even arise for such theories. For in such theories it is analytically true that beauty is enjoyable. Even a theory that takes, say, the medieval concept of "radiance" or, with Schiller, the notion of "living form"[37] as a criterion of beauty makes the connection between beauty and enjoyment understandable. For a term like "radiance" already implies such an attractiveness and allure that we could not wonder at liking whatever possessed it. And since we are told of "living form" that some living things do not have it, but that some inanimate things do, whatever it designates must already be so mysterious and such an object of awe and wonder that our attraction for it needs no explanation. But to say that beauty is the presence in an "object" to an extremely high degree of a property of qualitative degree is to say something so dry, colorless, and dispassionate that it must cause us to wonder that anything like *that* could ever be *enjoyed*.

The fact is, however, that beauty is enjoyable. Of course, it can be many other things too: pleasant, delightful, exhilarating, mind-blowing, and productive of ecstasy. It is different of these things to different people. And, as we all know, different beauties characteristically evoke different (positive) feelings. But even if all that is true, at least this much is also true: all beauty is in some way and in some degree *enjoyable*, and everyone *enjoys*, in some degree and at some times, beauty of some sort. And if we can explain, as we must, this minimal truth, it will be possible, at least in principle, to understand how beauty can be all those other things.

A minor point needs to be made before we begin the argument showing why beauty is enjoyable. "Beauty is enjoyable" is an elliptical way of saying that seeing, hearing, feeling, apprehending, etc., beauty is enjoyable. Strictly speaking, it is

[37] Adams (ed.), *Critical Theory Since Plato*, pp. 424ff.

the perceiving[38] of beauty that is enjoyable about beauty. This fact follows from a perfectly general truth about the use of "enjoy." If we enjoy a meal, it is *eating* the meal that we enjoy. If we enjoy gardens, it is *looking at* or *wandering through* gardens that we enjoy. When we enjoy music and art, we enjoy *listening to* or *playing* music and *looking at* or *studying* art. This point is elementary, but it is crucial to the argument that follows. What we must explain is why we enjoy perceiving an extremely high degree of any property of qualitative degree.

A second preliminary point is in order, too. Let us specify a bit more precisely what the proposition "perceiving beauty is enjoyable" means and does not mean and under what conditions it is true. First, perceiving beauty is enjoyable only when we notice or recognize the perceived beauty. For we may see or hear, in some acceptable senses of "see" and "hear," the beauty of some property without *recognizing* it as beautiful. Or, having once recognized the beauty in a thing, we might see that thing without paying any attention to its beauty. Or, having noticed the beauty of a thing many times, we might be so distracted by pain, worry, fear, or depression that it escapes our notice. In other words, "perceiving beauty" means "perceiving *and noticing* beauty" when we say that perceiving beauty is enjoyable. There is, moreover, a corollary to this proposition that goes: "Perceiving beauty is, generally speaking, more enjoyable than perceiving nonbeauty." Elaborated, this corollary means "Whenever we perceive (and notice) the high degree to which, for any X and F, X is F, our perception is, generally speaking, more enjoyable than whenever we perceive (and notice) the less-than-high degree to which, for any X and F, X is F, the domain of X being all 'objects' and the domain of

[38] I will use "perceive" as a generic term for all the modes of apprehending beauty.

F being all PQDs." I will attempt in the sequel to explain the facts expressed by the proposition and its corollary.

35. *An Explanation of the Enjoyment of Beauty*

The first premise of my explanation of these two facts is that *clearly* perceiving[39] the properties of an "object" is, generally speaking, enjoyable and more enjoyable than perceiving them with less-than-clarity. The reason, I think, that we say that a person *enjoys* good eyesight and good hearing is precisely because such things are, generally speaking, enjoyable. Naturally, most of the time when we see, hear, taste, or understand clearly, we do not feel thrills of enjoyment. For our enjoyment is felt, characteristically, whenever we have special occasion to notice or recognize the fact that we are perceiving clearly. For weeks after I got my first pair of glasses at the age of ten, I felt the enjoyment of seeing clearly: I had always thought it was normal to see everything with blurry outlines. Sometimes in viewing a film or slides we gradually feel our irritation and eyestrain until at last we notice that the image is slightly out of focus. When it is focussed clearly, there is a felt relief, a sense of lightening, a positive pleasure at being able to see clearly. The same is true when we are trying to get the point of an argument and are aware that our grasp of it is dim; there is pleasure when the light finally breaks through. Thus not only do we enjoy clear perception and understanding, but we enjoy them more than we enjoy perception and understanding that are less-than-clear; furthermore, we enjoy them under the same

[39] I take "perceive" in this context, as I did in the last section, to include "notice."

kinds of conditions as prevail when we enjoy beauty. I would not argue, however, that we enjoy clear perception to the same degree that we enjoy beauty. On the contrary, I think it is true, in general, that we enjoy beauty more than we enjoy perceiving clearly. For we can, after all, perceive a thing clearly, even though it is not beautiful. But if what we perceive clearly is, in addition, beautiful, our enjoyment will usually be compounded.

Let us imagine some cases of unclear perception of beautiful properties of things:

a) Suppose that you are taken out to your weekend host's garden during cocktail hour to admire his beautiful red parrot tulips. You are not particularly impressed, but you mutter something polite. The next morning, however, as you glance out into the garden you are stunned by the vividness of the red tulips. You figure that because of your alcohol content the previous evening you had not seen the color of the tulips clearly, and in particular had not seen how vivid it was.

b) Suppose that the first time you hear the Andromache theme from *Les Troyens* it seems to you sad, but not to have the ineffable sadness that you had been expecting from descriptions of it. Yet later you hear the same music, on the same recording, but on a different machine; and you hear for the first time how beautifully sad it is. You learn later that a small, barely detectable mechanical noise in the turntable of the first machine had the effect of "hardening" or "flattening" what you heard, so that the special expressiveness of the music could not come through clearly.

c) When your host hands you a glass of his scotch "discovery" and praises it as extra smooth, you know that you'll never be able to tell how smooth it is, for he's put ice in it. You're not able to taste the smoothness clearly enough. But the next time you're over, you're prepared to stop the ice, and the scotch turns out to be beautifully smooth indeed.

d) Imagine listening to a professional paper in a field or on a problem somewhere on the borders of your own interests and competence. Suppose that you know enough about the subject, both antecedently and from what you can piece together from the presentation itself, to perceive, if somewhat dimly, how imaginative the thesis of the paper is. You find it interesting and stimulating, but you do not, of course, know precisely how it fits into the traditions and contemporary work in its field. Imagine yourself becoming so interested that you get fairly heavily involved in that subject area yourself and come eventually to understand how very imaginative that paper had been.

e) Imagine a sunny, affable, open, honest, and direct neighbor who always knows what he thinks and who feels no hesitation letting others know it when, but only when, it is relevant and who, moreover, because of his quality of concerned forthrightness, never seems to offend anyone. Honesty in all its forms comes to him as second nature. You, however, are unable to be like your neighbor, are fearful of giving offense, are withdrawn and closed; and out of envy and meanness you are constantly finding petty faults in your neighbor. You grudgingly recognize his openness and honesty, but see him as too shallow and unreflective to appreciate the real awfulness and threatening character of the world, too optimistic to have thought very profoundly about things and, finally, just too lucky, because endowed with such a free and happy personality, really to merit being considered virtuous. You think he does not suffer enough to be virtuous. But then, by virtue of a psychoanalytic miracle, you are purged of your own anxieties and fears and come to see yourself and others clearly for the first time. You also recognize that it was simply your own meanness of spirit that had prevented you from understanding how truly beautiful your neighbor is in his utter honesty.

Let us summarize the common features in the preceding hypothetical situations. First, they all represent contrasts between perceiving a property of an "object" unclearly and perceiving it clearly. Second, all of the cases of unclear perception are cases in which a property is indeed perceived but only later perceived clearly. Furthermore, the cases of unclear perception are cases in which the property is perceived as having a *lower* degree when perceived unclearly than when perceived clearly. Let us here introduce the idea of the *apparent degree* of a property. The apparent degree of a property of an "object" is the degree the property of that "object" is perceived as having, whether the perception is clear or less-than-clear. Thus, for example, when I perceive the beautiful delicacy of a leaf pattern with great clarity, the apparent degree of delicacy in that act of seeing is extremely high. In all of the five hypothetical situations the apparent degree of the respective properties when perceived unclearly is somewhat lower than the apparent degree of those properties as later perceived clearly.

Now whenever a PQD is perceived less-than-clearly, it always has, in that act of apprehension, a lower apparent degree than it would have in an act of *clear* perception of that same PQD in that same "object." The argument for this assertion is as follows. When we perceive PQDs less-than-clearly, we nevertheless perceive them. But the difference between the way they appear to us when we apprehend them clearly and when we apprehend them unclearly can only be in their apparent degrees. Thus it is that whenever we apprehend X's F (where F is a PQD) less-than-clearly, we do not apprehend just how F X is. The sentence form *"I did not see just how F X is,"* used when I reflect on my unclear perception, never suggests that I perceived X as having a higher degree of F than it has, but always implies that in my unclear perception the apparent degree of F was lower than it is in fact. This is so, not because we never apprehend the F of X as having a degree higher than it has, but because when we do the F is not properly described as "less-than-clearly perceived."

In my drunkenness the fineness of a woman's features may appear to me greater than what they are in fact. Or my hasty glance may not have noticed her blemished skin, or I may have seen her through the gauze curtains on the window, which hide her wrinkles. In such circumstances the liquor, the haste, or the gauze may make me see the woman's face unclearly, her features unclearly, or her skin unclearly; but they do not make me see her fineness of features unclearly, the clearness of her skin unclearly, or the freshness of her face unclearly, when what is meant is that her features are not very fine, her face not very fresh, or her skin not very clear. What these circumstances do is to give me something like *illusions*, not unclear perceptions. For what happens is that I perceive something as "there," namely, a high degree of some PQD, which high degree does not exist "there." On the other hand, when we perceive F less-than-clearly by perceiving F as having a lower degree than it actually has, it is not, our intuitions tell us, that we perceive what is not "there." For we feel that degrees are, in general, cumulative—even the degrees of PQDs. Just as, when there are one hundred degrees of heat in the water, we know that there are at least ninety degrees there, so when X possesses F to a high degree, we know that X possesses F at least to a moderate degree. I am not saying that this comparison between two sorts of degrees is well founded. I present it only to show how we *suppose* properties of degree to work. For we can thereby explain how it is that when the apparent degree of a property of an "object" is greater than the degree of that property actually is, we treat the experience of that apparent degree as we do an illusion, and when the apparent degree is less than it actually is, we treat the experience as a case of less-than-clear perception.

We may conclude, then, that perceiving X's F clearly, when F ranges only over PQDs, is just perceiving F in such a way that the apparent degree of F is not significantly lower than the degree that X's F actually has, and, of course, is not higher either. But note that beauty with respect to any F is the degree range of F from extremely high on up. Therefore, perceiving X's beauty with respect to F must be perceiving X's F in such a way that the apparent degree of F is not significantly lower than what X's F actually has, and is not much higher either. For X could not possess F to a degree much higher than it appears to, if F is already apprehended as beautiful, that is, as having an extremely high degree. From this fact it follows that perceiving beauty is a special case of clear perception. And since perceiving clearly is enjoyable, so is perceiving beauty.[40]

[40] It is also true that the greater the degree in which F is present in X, the clearer the perception of F is. Thus perceiving the high degree of any F is always perceiving F with very great clarity, which means that we always perceive beauty *beautifully*, that is, with a beautiful clarity.

A necessary condition of perceiving beauty is hence being beautiful in some respect. This unforeseen consequence of NTB in some way illuminates an idea of Plotinus's I've always found puzzling:

"To any vision must be brought an eye adapted to what is to be seen and having some likeness to it. Never did eye see sun unless it had first become sun-like, and never can the soul have vision of the First Beauty unless itself be beautiful." *The Enneads*, tr. Stephen MacKenna, 3rd ed. (New York: Pantheon, n.d.) p. 65.

Plotinus, to be sure, has moral beauty primarily in mind in this passage, whereas my point applies merely to being "intellectually" beautiful. It is plausible, however, that Plotinus was led to this view

36. *Surpassing Clarity*

The preceding explanation of why we enjoy beauty, though interesting and, as far as I know, novel, is not quite sufficient, however. For we still want to know why perceiving beauty should be *especially* enjoyable—more enjoyable, on the whole, than the ordinary clear perception of the less-than-beautiful. The answer to this question will make use of points established in the preceding section.

If one perceives X's F, and X's F has no beauty in it, then the apparent degree of X's F is lower than the apparent degree of F when one perceives the beauty of Y with respect to F. Now it is theoretically possible for the apparent degree of X's (unbeautiful) F when perceived clearly to be equal to the apparent degree of Y's (beautiful) F when perceived *unclearly*. Therefore, in the crucial respect of the "apparent degree" of the perceived property, (clearly) perceiving the beauty of Y's (beautiful) F compares to perceiving unclearly Y's (beautiful) F as (clearly) perceiving Y's (beautiful) F compares to clearly perceiving X's (unbeautiful) F. And thus, too, the clear perception of beauty vis-à-vis ordinary clear perception is strictly analogous to the clear perception of a thing's (not necessarily beautiful) PQD vis-à-vis the unclear perception of that same PQD whether instantiated in that thing or some other thing. Furthermore, the analogy depends precisely on the way that perceived PQDs appear to the perceiver—on what the acts of

---

precisely because he intuited the necessary connections between beauty in "objects" and beauty in the perception of them. In any case it is not even implausible that Plotinus is right in thinking that moral beauty in the perceiver is a prerequisite to perceiving moral beauty in others. I know of no way of verifying the claim, however.

perception "look like" on the "inside," as it were. Therefore, our perception of beauty with respect to some *F* is *to us as if* we were perceiving *F extraordinarily* clearly.

I emphasize that, while the perception of beauty is necessarily clear perception, it is not perception that is, literally speaking, more clear than the ordinary clear perception of ordinary, less-than-beautiful properties. It is merely that, in our *experience* of beauty, it *seems to us as if* perceiving beauty is as much clearer than ordinary clear perception of nonbeauty as such ordinary clear perception of nonbeauty is clearer than the less-than-clear perception of nonbeauty. And, therefore, since clear perception is generally more enjoyable than perception that is less-than-clear, perceiving beauty is more enjoyable to us, in general, than the ordinary clear perception of the less-than-beautiful. The perception of beauty is always clear perception but also, *as it were*, clearer than clear perception.

At this point it is important to take stock of what exactly has been explained. Note that we have been explaining why, *in general*, perceiving beauty is enjoyable and why, *in general*, it is more enjoyable than ordinary clear perception. The italicized qualifying phrase is important because it means that from the preceding explanations we cannot *conclude* that *every* case of perceiving beauty is either enjoyable or more enjoyable than cases of ordinary clear perceiving. Indeed, were we able so to conclude, the explanations would be faulty, for it simply is not true that perceiving beauty is *always* enjoyable. The enjoyment of beauty, as of anything else, depends upon many factors in our own mental makeup, our personal associations and history, our temporary state of mind. The most, then, that the preceding explanations can tell us is that any case of perceiving beauty will be enjoyable, and more enjoyable than a case of perceiving nonbeauty, *as long as there are no factors in the situa-*

tion that cause displeasure or other discomfort sufficient to outweigh the enjoyment arising from (1) perceiving clearly and (2) seeming to perceive "more clearly than clearly."

The preceding qualification is exceedingly important because the above explanations of our enjoyment of beauty in fact explain more than our enjoyment of beauty. They explain our enjoyment of the high degree of any PQD. But beauty is not simply the high degree of just any PQD, but only of those that are not properties of deficiency, defect, or lack or of the "appearance" of deficiency, defect, or lack. Without the above italicized qualifying clause, in other words, we should, according to the above explanations, enjoy perceiving high degrees of evil, corruption, stupidity, and hideousness; but, in general, we do not. Yet even with the qualifying clause it seems to be a consequence of the preceding explanations that at least *in some respect*, even if not usually an overriding respect, the perception of a very high degree of properties like evil, corruption, stupidity, and hideousness is enjoyable.

But this consequence does not embarrass the theory; on the contrary, it provides corroboration for it. It has long been puzzling, not only to philosophers but also to people, why we are so ("perversely") attracted to, so ("morbidly") fascinated by, extremes of nonbeauty, by "ugliness" of many sorts. Now we know the solution. We actually enjoy perceiving "ugliness" precisely in that respect in which we enjoy perceiving beauty. But, you might ask, how can that be? For it is obvious that we enjoy perceiving beauty so much *more* than perceiving "ugliness" and that most of us most of the time simply do *not* enjoy perceiving "ugliness." True, and the reason for that is also obvious. In the perception of varieties of ugliness the factors—which hardly need cataloging here—causing displeasure and other forms of discomfort are usually, and for

137

most people, sufficient to outweigh the enjoyment arising from (1) clarity of perception and (2) the appearance of perceiving "more clearly than clearly."

We might ask, of course, why in the first place it should be enjoyable to perceive clearly. I don't know for sure, and it would take me too long to try to answer that question here and now. I suspect, though, that it has to do with (1) knowing exactly what our immediate environment (or a part of it) is like and (2) feeling that our faculties are in excellent order. These in turn are enjoyable because, having optimum access to our world and feeling our faculties working well, we feel perfectly equipped to operate in that world. In short, we feel very well off in such circumstances. Remember that this is mere speculation (but speculation that I can't resist). Yet if this speculation is anywhere near the truth, then we ultimately enjoy beauty because in perceiving beauty we seem to be *better* off than merely very well off. For in perceiving beauty we seem to be perceiving with a much greater degree of clarity than our ordinary clear perception has. In perceiving beauty we are filled, if only for a moment and if only in a limited respect, by a feeling of transcendent well-being.

INDEX